relax Kids

The Dream Machine

Create your own Magical Adventures
By Marneta Viegas

Illustrations by Nicola Wyldbore-Smith
& Sarah Adams
Design by Amber Sutton

OUR STREET
BOOKS

Winchester, UK
Washington, USA

JOHN HUNT PUBLISHING

First published by Our Street Books, 2021
Our Street Books is an imprint of John Hunt Publishing Ltd., Laurel House, Station Approach,
Alresford, Hants, SO24 9JH, UK
office@jhpbooks.net
www.johnhuntpublishing.com
www.ourstreet-books.com

For distributor details and how to order please visit the 'Ordering' section on our website.

Text copyright: Marneta Viegas 2017
Illustrations: Nicola Wyldbore-Smith
Sarah Adams
Design: Amber Sutton

ISBN: 978 1 78904 998 5
978 1 78904 999 2 (ebook)
Library of Congress Control Number: 2021942630

Printed by: Gutenberg Press Ltd - Gudja Road, Tarxien GXQ 2902 Malta

We operate a distinctive and ethical publishing philosophy in
all areas of our business, from our global network of authors to
production and worldwide distribution.

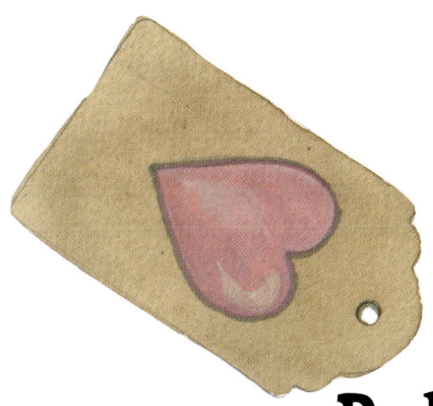

Dedication:

This book is dedicated to my beautiful sister Maria.
She was such an adventurer as we were growing up and was always having adventures with mud at the bottom of the garden.
Maria always dreamt of being a fire fighter.
One day, after lots of hard work, her dream came true.
She is an inspiration - you can be whatever you want to be.

"In an ever increasing digital world, books like this are so important and wonderful for the imagination......Sweeter than the sweetest sweet in a sweet shop." **DOM WOOD - CBBC**

CONTENTS PAGE

Page 3 Enter the Portal

Page 5 Yellow Haze

Page 7 Orange Haze

Page 9 Green Smoke Portal

Page 11 Purple Sky Portal

Page 13 Blue Glass Portal

Page 15 Silver Dew Portal

Page 17 White Swirl Portal

Page 19 Amber Portal

Page 21 Indigo Mirror Portal

Page 23 Aqua Cloud Portal

Page 25 Magic Carpet

Page 27 Private Jet

Page 29 Unicorn

Page 31 Hot Air Balloon

Page 33 Time Machine

Page 35 Invisibility Dust

Page 37 Boat

Page 39 Hover Board

Page 41 Broomstick

Page 43 Rocket

Page 45 Magical Mountain

Page 47 Lake of Enchantment

Page 49 Woods of Mystery

Page 51 Secret Garden

Page 53 Shimmering Sea

Page 55 Whispering Grassland

Page 57 Unknown Wilderness

Page 59 Rainbow Waterfall

Page 61 Sleepy Streams

Page 63 Ancient Island

Page 65 Red Door

Page 67 Blue Door

Page 69 Green Door

Page 71 Pink Door

Page 73 Stone Door

Page 75 Orange Door

Page 77 Golden Door

Page 79 White Door

Page 81 Silver Door

Page 83 Rainbow Door

Page 85 Cave of Calm

Page 87 Hut of Happiness

Page 89 Den of Dreams

Page 91 House of Hearts

Page 93 Tower of Power

Page 95 Well of Wishes
Page 97 Castle of Creativity
Page 99 Room of Rest
Page 101 Maze of Miracles
Page 103 Palace of Peace
Page 105 Wise Man
Page 107 Angel
Page 109 Wizard
Page 111 Elf
Page 113 Fortune Teller
Page 115 Genie
Page 117 Queen of Hearts
Page 119 Spirit Guide
Page 121 Goddess
Page 123 Superhero
Page 125 Diamond
Page 127 Heart
Page 129 Leaf
Page 131 Circle
Page 133 Star
Page 135 Triangle
Page 137 Flower
Page 139 Spiral

Page 141 Sun
Page 143 Moon
Page 146 Number 01
Page 148 Number 02
Page 150 Number 03
Page 152 Number 04
Page 154 Number 05
Page 156 Number 06
Page 158 Number 07
Page 160 Numbe 08
Page 162 Number 09
Page 164 Number 10
Page 166 Plum Key
Page 168 Orange Key
Page 170 Purple Key
Page 172 Pink Key
Page 174 Black Key
Page 176 White Key
Page 178 Green Key
Page 180 Aqua Key
Page 182 Yellow Key
Page 184 Blue Key
Page 186 The End

Foreword

I was really excited to get the chance to read this book because I love it when Relax Kids brings out a new book! This book is especially exciting because it's not like normal books where you read the story from start to finish. It's not like reading the same book over and over again; you can make up different adventures each time. There is a purple trail to follow and as you read, you start to really feel as if you are going through the portal. You can choose different adventures, depending on how you are feeling. For example, if you are worried about the future, you might choose to meet the Fortune Teller. If you are going to bed but don't feel tired, you could choose to visit the Sleepy Streams. I like that there are spaces to draw your own pictures of what your "Den of dreams" or "Room of rest" look like. This makes it feel more like **YOUR** own unique book. I love the pictures, which help your imagination as you read. The pages of the book feel really nice too. I think that this book is for both boys and girls and adults, too!. It's a great book to have, because it can help you feel calmer (like before exciting things like Christmas or Birthdays!), braver, kinder and more confident.

Thank you, Relax Kids.

Emily Marek, age 8

From Marneta

This is a meditation book where you are the star in your own story and can choose where you want to go. You are always in control and you can go back through the portal and back in the room whenever you wish.
There are thousands of combinations and each time you go on an adventure, it will be different.

I have included some NLP (Neuro-Linguistic Programming),
EFT (Emotional Freedom Technique - tapping) and positive affirmation techniques in the visualizations as well as mentioning crystal healing, aromatherapy/herbs and color therapy. These are becoming more popular as we are collecting tools to help us feel more calm and relaxed. However, just do what you feel comfortable with.

Remember that you are always in control.
You are the master adventurer. Have a wonderful time adventuring into the amazing world of your imagination.

Start reading here,
follow the purple
path

Remember you are completely in control.
You are incharge of your adventure

Over the page are 10 colored portals. Turn the page to choose a
portal. Choose a color, then feel yourself stepping through the
portal. You could imagine you are stepping through a mirror,
a tube or going through a slide, trap door or even a mist of
swirling colored light.

The more times you step through to the portal of your
imagination, the more opportunities you will have to
collect valuable messages, symbols and gifts that will help
you feel more calm, positive and confident.

Each time you go through the portal,
you could have any one of a hundred
thousand different experiences.

Are you ready to step through the portal of
your imagination?

Magical Adventurer

WELCOME

ENTER THE PORTAL HERE

Close your eyes,

be very still and relax.

To go through the YELLOW HAZE PORTAL – turn to page 5

To go through the ORANGE THUNDER PORTAL – Turn to page 7

To go through the SILVER DEW PORTAL – Turn to page 15

To go through the INDIGO MIRROR PORTAL – Turn to page 21

turn to page 5

Turn to page 7

Turn to page 15

Turn to page 21

Stand in front of your chosen portal and feel yourself gently disappearing from the room, and entering the magical portal of your imagination.

To go through the GREEN SMOKE PORTAL - turn to page 9

To go through the PURPLE SKY PORTAL - Turn to page 11

To go through the AQUA CLOUD PORTAL - Turn to page 23

To go through the BLUE GLASS PORTAL - Turn to page 13

To go through the AMBER PORTAL - Turn to page 19

To go through the WHITE SWIRL PORTAL - Turn to page 17

THE YELLOW HAZE PORTAL

Start

Welcome, Magical Adventurer to the YELLOW HAZE PORTAL. Take in a deep breath all the way to your fingers and toes, and let it out as slowly and gently as you can. Squeeze your toes as hard as you can and then gently let them go and relax. Squeeze your legs and then let them go until they feel soft and relaxed like a rag doll.

Pull in your tummy as tight as you can and slowly let it go until it feels completely relaxed. Squeeze your arms and lift your shoulders up to your ears and let them go.

To fly on a MAGIC CARPET, turn to page 25
To travel in a PRIVATE JET, turn to page 27
To fly on your own UNICORN, turn to page 29
To travel in a HOT AIR BALLOON, turn to page 31
To travel in a TIME MACHINE, turn to page 33
To use magic INVISIBILITY DUST, turn to page 35
To travel by BOAT, turn to page 37
To fly on a HOVER BOARD, turn to page 39
To fly on a BROOMSTICK, turn to page 41
To travel in a ROCKET, turn to page 43

You are about to go on a magical adventure.

On this adventure you will meet special people, receive gifts and messages and be shown some great exercises to help you feel calm and confident.

Relax

THE ORANGE THUNDER PORTAL

Take in a deep breath all the way to your fingers and toes, and let it out as slowly and gently as you can.

ORANGE THUNDER PORTAL.

Stretch your face as wide as you can and relax.

Welcome, Magical Adventurer to the

Start

Raise your eyebrows and stretch your forehead as high as you can and relax. Stretch your nose and mouth as wide as you can and relax. Can you stretch your ears? Open your ears wide and stretch. Now relax your whole face. See if you can make your face floppy. Feel your eyes sinking to the back of your head.

Just let go and relax

relax

relax

You are about to go on a magical adventure.

On this adventure you will meet special people, receive gifts and messages and be shown some great exercises to help you feel calm and confident.

HOW WOULD YOU LIKE TO BE TRANSPORTED TO YOUR MAGICAL ADVENTURE?

To fly on a MAGIC CARPET, turn to **page 25**
To travel in a PRIVATE JET, turn to **page 27**
To fly on your own UNICORN, turn to **page 29**
To travel in a HOT AIR BALLOON, turn to page 31
To travel in a TIME MACHINE, turn to **page 33**
To use magic INVISIBILITY DUST, turn to page 35
To travel by BOAT, turn to **page 37**
To fly on a HOVER BOARD, turn to **page 39**
To fly on a BROOMSTICK, turn to **page 41**
To travel in a ROCKET, turn to **page 43**

THE GREEN SMOKE PORTAL

Start

Welcome, Magical Adventurer to the GREEN SMOKE PORTAL. Take in a deep breath all the way to your fingers and toes, and let it out as slowly and gently as you can. Feel your stomach rising as you breathe in. Take in a deep breath all the way into your stomach. Feel your stomach. HOLD YOUR BREATHE FOR A COUPLE OF SECONDS

and very slowly breathe out with a soft, slow, steady breath. Breathe in as slowly as you can and breathe out even slower and even softer. Breathe in...... and breathe out.

On this adventure you will meet special people, receive gifts and messages and be shown some great exercises to help you feel calm and confident.

HOW WOULD YOU LIKE TO BE TRANSPORTED TO YOUR MAGICAL ADVENTURE?

You are about to go on a magical adventure.

To fly on a MAGIC CARPET, turn to page 25
To travel in a PRIVATE JET, turn to page 27
To fly on your own UNICORN, turn to page 29
To travel in a HOT AIR BALLOON, turn to page 31
To travel in a TIME MACHINE, turn to page 33
To use magic INVISIBILITY DUST, turn to page 35
To travel by BOAT, turn to page 37
To fly on a HOVER BOARD, turn to page 39
To fly on a BROOMSTICK, turn to page 41
To travel in a ROCKET, turn to page 43

THE PURPLE SKY PORTAL

Welcome, Magical Adventurer to the PURPLE SKY PORTAL. Take in a deep breath all the way to your fingers and toes, and let it out as slowly and gently as you can... Feel your feet becoming heavy and relaxed, and feel them slowly sinking downwards. Feel the muscles in your feet uncurling and unwinding. Feel them becoming heavier and heavier.

Start

Just let them go and relax. Let your legs become heavy and sink downwards. Relax your ankles, calves, shins, backs of your knees and thighs. Feel your spine sinking deeply into the ground. Feel your arms becoming heavy and sinking. Let your head become heavy and sink down. Feel your eyes becoming heavy, relax the tiny muscles at the back of the eyes and let your eyebrows sink gently into your head. Feel your whole body becoming heavy and relaxed.

To fly on a MAGIC CARPET, turn to page 25
To travel in a PRIVATE JET, turn to page 27
To fly on your own UNICORN, turn to page 29
To travel in a HOT AIR BALLOON, turn to page 31
To travel in a TIME MACHINE, turn to page 33
To use magic INVISIBILITY DUST, turn to page 35
To travel by BOAT, turn to page 37
To fly on a HOVER BOARD, turn to page 39
To fly on a BROOMSTICK, turn to page 41
To travel in a ROCKET, turn to page 43

HOW WOULD YOU LIKE TO BE TRANSPORTED TO YOUR MAGICAL ADVENTURE?

On this adventure you will meet special people, receive gifts and messages and be shown some great exercises to help you feel calm and confident.

You are about to go on a magical adventure.

THE BLUE GLASS PORTAL

Stretch -- Stretch -- Stretch

Stretch

Stretch from the top of your head to the tip of your toes.

Take in a deep breath all the way to your fingers and toes, and let it out as slowly and gently as you can.

BLUE GLASS PORTAL

Start

Welcome, Magical Adventurer to the

Stretch your whole body like a big elastic band.

When you can stretch no more, let the elastic band go and relax. Feel your whole body letting go and relaxing completely. Stretch one more time. Stretch, stretch, stretch and let go and relax like a floppy elastic band.

How would you like to be transported to your magical adventure?

To fly on a MAGIC CARPET, turn to page 25
To travel in a PRIVATE JET, turn to page 27
To fly on your own UNICORN, turn to page 29
To travel in a HOT AIR BALLOON, turn to page 31
To travel in a TIME MACHINE, turn to page 33
To use magic INVISIBILITY DUST, turn to page 35
To travel by BOAT, turn to page 37
To fly on a HOVER BOARD, turn to page 39
To fly on a BROOMSTICK, turn to page 41
To travel in a ROCKET, turn to page 43

You are about to go on a magical adventure.

On this adventure you will meet special people, receive gifts and messages and be shown some great exercises to help you feel calm and confident.

THE SILVER DEW PORTAL

Say to yourself slowly. I am peaceful, I am peaceful, I am peaceful, I am peaceful.

Welcome, Magical Adventurer to the SILVER DEW PORTAL. Take in a deep breath all the way to your fingers and toes, and let it out as slowly and gently as you can.

Start

Feel your face becoming peaceful and quiet. Feel your neck becoming peaceful and relaxed. Feel your chest becoming peaceful.
Feel your arms becoming peaceful. Feel your back becoming peaceful.
Feel the peace moving to your legs and feet. Notice how peaceful your whole body feels.

How would you like to be transported to your magical adventure?

To fly on a MAGIC CARPET, turn to page 25
To travel in a PRIVATE JET, turn to page 27
To fly on your own UNICORN, turn to page 29
To travel in a HOT AIR BALLOON, turn to page 31
To travel in a TIME MACHINE, turn to page 33
To use magic INVISIBILITY DUST, turn to page 35
To travel by BOAT, turn to page 37
To fly on a HOVER BOARD, turn to page 39
To fly on a BROOMSTICK, turn to page 41
To travel in a ROCKET, turn to page 43

You are about to go on a magical adventure.

On this adventure you will meet special people, receive gifts and messages and be shown some great exercises to help you feel calm and confident.

THE WHITE SWIRL PORTAL

WHITE SWIRL PORTAL.

Start

Welcome, Magical Adventurer to the WHITE SWIRL PORTAL.

Take in a deep breath all the way to your fingers and toes, and let it out as slowly and gently as you can.

Spend some time listening to all the sounds inside the room.

Stay very still and quiet and listen to any sounds outside the room. The more still and quiet you are, the more you will be aware of the sounds around you.

You are about to go on a magical adventure.

On this adventure you will meet special people, receive gifts and messages and be shown some great exercises to help you feel calm and confident.

How would you like to be transported to your magical adventure?

To fly on a MAGIC CARPET, turn to page 25
To travel in a PRIVATE JET, turn to page 27
To fly on your own UNICORN, turn to page 29
To travel in a HOT AIR BALLOON, turn to page 31
To travel in a TIME MACHINE, turn to page 33
To use magic INVISIBILITY DUST, turn to page 35
To travel by BOAT, turn to page 37
To fly on a HOVER BOARD, turn to page 39
To fly on a BROOMSTICK, turn to page 41
To travel in a ROCKET, turn to page 43

THE AMBER PORTAL

Start

Welcome, Magical Adventurer to the AMBER PORTAL. Take in a deep breath all the way to your fingers and toes, and let it out as slowly and gently as you can. Stay there very still. As you stay still, take in a deep breath.

As you breathe in, breathe in a feeling of peace. As you breathe out, breathe out a feeling of peace, breathe in peace, breathe out peace. You feel so safe and cozy here, so just allow all your thoughts to slow down gently while you enjoy the peace and quiet.

To fly on a MAGIC CARPET, turn to page 25
To travel in a PRIVATE JET, turn to page 27
To fly on your own UNICORN, turn to page 29
To travel in a HOT AIR BALLOON, turn to page 31
To travel in a TIME MACHINE, turn to page 33
To use magic INVISIBILITY DUST, turn to page 35
To travel by BOAT, turn to page 37
To fly on a HOVER BOARD, turn to page 39
To fly on a BROOMSTICK, turn to page 41
To travel in a ROCKET, turn to page 43

HOW WOULD YOU LIKE TO BE TRANSPORTED TO YOUR MAGICAL ADVENTURE?

On this adventure you will meet special people, receive gifts and messages and be shown some great exercises to help you feel calm and confident.

You are about to go on a magical adventure.

THE INDIGO MIRROR PORTAL

How tiny can you make your fists?

and let it out as slowly and gently as you can,

How tiny can you make your fists?

to your fingers and toes,

all the way to your fingers and toes,

INDIGO MIRROR PORTAL

Start

Welcome, Magical Adventurer to the INDIGO MIRROR PORTAL

Take in a deep breath

see if you can make each fist into a tiny ball.

Squeeze your fists as tight as you can,

Squeeze, squeeze and now uncurl your **fingers** very, very **slowly** and relax your hands, let them drop down **and** become **heavy**.
Try that again. Put all your stress and **tension** into you**r fists** and squeeze them as much as you possibly can. Squeeze, squeeze, squeeze and relax. Uncurl your fingers and feel them almost float as you uncurl them

HOW WOULD YOU LIKE TO BE TRANSPORTED TO YOUR MAGICAL ADVENTURE?

To fly on a MAGIC CARPET, turn to page 25
To travel in a PRIVATE JET, turn to page 27
To fly on your own UNICORN, turn to page 29
To travel in a HOT AIR BALLOON, turn to page 31
To travel in a TIME MACHINE, turn to page 33
To use magic INVISIBILITY DUST, turn to page 35
To travel by BOAT, turn to page 37
To fly on a HOVER BOARD, turn to page 39
To fly on a BROOMSTICK, turn to page 41
To travel in a ROCKET, turn to page 43

On this adventure you will meet special people, receive gifts and messages and be shown some great exercises to help you feel calm and confident.

You are about to go on a magical adventure

THE AQUA PORTAL

Welcome, Magical Adventurer to the AQUA CLOUD PORTAL. Take in a deep breath all the way to your fingers and toes, and let it out as slowly and gently as you can. Imagine the path beneath you is warm and you are melting gently into the floor.

Start

Feel your whole body becoming soft and gooey as you melt and relax into the floor. Feel your whole body turning to liquid as you soften and relax into the floor. Stay there, soft and relaxed.

You are about to go on a magical adventure.

On this adventure you will meet special people, receive gifts and messages and be shown some great exercises to help you feel calm and confident.

HOW WOULD YOU LIKE TO BE TRANSPORTED TO YOUR MAGICAL ADVENTURE?

To fly on a MAGIC CARPET, turn to **page 25**
To travel in a PRIVATE JET, turn to **page 27**
To fly on your own UNICORN, turn to **page 29**
To travel in a HOT AIR BALLOON, turn to page 31
To travel in a TIME MACHINE, turn to page 33
To use magic INVISIBILITY DUST, turn to page 35
To travel by BOAT, turn to page 37
To fly on a HOVER BOARD, turn to page 39
To fly on a BROOMSTICK, turn to page 41
To travel in a ROCKET, turn to page 43

Sit in the middle of your

MAGIC CARPET

and cross your legs. Say the magic word

ABRACADABRA

START HERE

And now, the carpet picks up a little speed and you start to move forward. You can swoop and soar, dip and dive, zip and zoom. The tassels of the carpet are blowing in the wind, feel the air rushing through your hair and the clouds brushing your face.

You feel fresh and invigorated as the magic carpet takes you around the world.

and feel the carpet start to float very gently above the ground. Feel yourself getting lighter and lighter as you fly higher into the air, up and up you go until you are far into the clouds.

When you are ready, ask the carpet to slow down or float as you stop to look at the magnificent landscapes below.

To go to the MAGICAL MOUNTAIN, turn to page 45
To go to the LAKE OF ENCHANTMENT, turn to page 47
To go to the WOODS OF MYSTERY, turn to page 49
To visit the SECRET GARDEN, turn to page 51
To visit the SHIMMERING SEA, turn to page 53
To go to the WHISPERING GRASSLAND, turn to page 55
To visit the UNKNOWN WILDERNESS, turn to page 57
To visit the RAINBOW WATERFALL, turn to page 59
To go to the SLEEPY STREAMS, turn to page 61
To go to the ANCIENT ISLAND, turn to page 63

Fasten your seat belt and relax back into the comfortable seat. The pilot makes an announcement letting you know that you are about to take off.

Step into your PRIVATE JET

START HERE

Feel the jet moving forward and picking up speed.
You can see you are moving fast along the runway.
All of a sudden the jet takes off into the air.
Your stomach gives a little flutter as you take off into the air.

Feel the jet soaring through the sky, getting higher and higher. After a while, you find yourself cruising at a high altitude.

Relax and enjoy your drink and snack as you fly through the air to your destination. In the screen in front of you there is a choice of destinations.

You can choose which one you would like. Make your choice and feel the jet take you to the destination of your choice.

To go to the MAGICAL MOUNTAIN, turn to page 45
To go to the LAKE OF ENCHANTMENT, turn to page 47
To go to the WOODS OF MYSTERY, turn to page 49
To visit the SECRET GARDEN, turn to page 51
To visit the SHIMMERING SEA, turn to page 53
To go to the WHISPERING GRASSLAND, turn to page 55
To visit the UNKNOWN WILDERNESS, turn to page 57
To visit the RAINBOW WATERFALL, turn to page 59
To go to the SLEEPY STREAMS, turn to page 61
To go to the ANCIENT ISLAND, turn to page 63

Climb up onto your beautiful white UNICORN

It runs faster and faster until suddenly its wings start to flap and it is flying gracefully in the air.
Hold tight onto the rainbow mane as you feel the wind on your face and the air rushing through your hair.

You feel so happy as you fly through the air

You feel light and free.

When you are ready, let your magic Unicorn take you to the next step of your magical adventure.

Stroke the Unicorn's horn. It is sparkling in the sunshine.

Hold on tight and whisper in your Unicorn's ear. The Unicorn nods and stamps its feet before starting to run.

To go to the MAGICAL MOUNTAIN, turn to page 45
To go to the LAKE OF ENCHANTMENT, turn to page 47
To go to the WOODS OF MYSTERY, turn to page 49
To visit the SECRET GARDEN, turn to page 51
To visit the SHIMMERING SEA, turn to page 53
To go to the WHISPERING GRASSLAND, turn to page 55
To visit the UNKNOWN WILDERNESS, turn to page 57
To visit the RAINBOW WATERFALL, turn to page 59
To go to the SLEEPY STREAMS, turn to page 61
To go to the ANCIENT ISLAND, turn to page 63

HOT AIR BALLOON

Stand up in your

The balloon is rising softly into the air.
You feel light and weightless as you rise higher into the sky.
Your whole body feels light and free.
All your muscles are relaxed and soft.

You feel so happy and free as you glide upwards into the clouds. Feel the warm breeze on your face as you drift through the air. Your eyes feel relaxed. Your ears are relaxed. Your cheeks are soft and relaxed. Your mouth is soft and relaxed.

You feel your hair blowing softly in the warm wind.

Look down below and see a hazy picture of rivers and patchwork fields. You see cornfields and green fields and fields of blue lavender and red poppies. You see gentle hills with tiny white sheep grazing peacefully.

You can see the rivers lazily meandering through the countryside. The sight is spectacular.

You are starting to glide gently towards the ground. Where are you going next? Where is the balloon taking you?

To go to the **MAGICAL MOUNTAIN**, turn to page 45
To go to the **LAKE OF ENCHANTMENT**, turn to page 47
To go to the **WOODS OF MYSTERY**, turn to page 49
To visit the **SECRET GARDEN**, turn to page 51
To visit the **SHIMMERING SEA**, turn to page 53
To go to the **WHISPERING GRASSLAND**, turn to page 55
To visit the **UNKNOWN WILDERNESS**, turn to page 57
To visit the **RAINBOW WATERFALL**, turn to page 59
To go to the **SLEEPY STREAMS**, turn to page 61
To go to the **ANCIENT ISLAND**, turn to page 63

Step inside the TIME MACHINE...

Take some time to listen to all the sounds around you.
It is very quiet here. All the sounds from outside are shut out and
you can only hear the low hum of the machine in standby and the
sound of your breathing. Take a moment to enjoy the quiet.
Sit down and put on your seat belt. It is time to start the
machine. Can you see the big red lever right above your
head? Pull it down. In front of you are lots of multi-colored
buttons and switches.

Where are you going next?

Where would you like to go?

To go to the **MAGICAL MOUNTAIN**, turn to page 45
To go to the **LAKE OF ENCHANTMENT**, turn to page 47
To go to the **WOODS OF MYSTERY**, turn to page 49
To visit the **SECRET GARDEN**, turn to page 51
To visit the **SHIMMERING SEA**, turn to page 53
To go to the **WHISPERING GRASSLAND**, turn to page 55
To visit the **UNKNOWN WILDERNESS**, turn to page 57
To visit the **RAINBOW WATERFALL**, turn to page 59
To go to the **SLEEPY STREAMS**, turn to page 61
To go to the **ANCIENT ISLAND**, turn to page 63

START HERE

There are pictures and numbers on each button.
On each picture is a different time and place in history.
You can visit wherever you want to go. Press a button to activate the time machine and hold tight onto your seat as the time machine whizzes and whirs into action. You can feel your whole body moving as you are catapulted backwards through space and time.

It is an invigorating feeling.

You feel totally safe and secure in the huge machine.
You don't need to worry about anything. In a minute, the machine will come to a gentle standstill. You will have arrived at the next stage of your exciting adventure.

Hold your bottle of **INVISIBILITY DUST.**

invisibility dust...

jar of Calm

START HERE

Where would you like to go next? The choice is yours.

To go to the MAGICAL MOUNTAIN, turn to page 45
To go to the LAKE OF ENCHANTMENT, turn to page 47
To go to the WOODS OF MYSTERY, turn to page 49
To visit the SECRET GARDEN, turn to page 51
To visit the SHIMMERING SEA, turn to page 53
To go to the WHISPERING GRASSLAND, turn to page 55
To visit the UNKNOWN WILDERNESS, turn to page 57
To visit the RAINBOW WATERFALL, turn to page 59
To go to the SLEEPY STREAMS, turn to page 61
To go to the ANCIENT ISLAND, turn to page 63

This will allow you to become invisible and travel anywhere without being seen. Sprinkle the dust over your feet and notice them fading away and becoming invisible. Sprinkle the dust on your legs and they become invisible. Sprinkle dust on your chest and down your back and they become invisible. Sprinkle the dust on your arms and finally your head.

You are completely

invisible.

invisibility dust...

You feel completely light and free. You can move through the air without being heard or seen. You feel a sense of excitement at being able to go anywhere you wish without being seen.

Sit in your

BOAT

The water is very calm and you are gently bobbing up and down as the wind carries you along.

START HERE

Lie down in the boat and feel the Sun on your face. You can smell the fresh smell of sea air. The boat is quietly rocking from side to side, the breeze softly billows the sails of the boat.

You feel so free

Your body is relaxed, your mind is light. You are carefree without a single worry in the world. Everything is quiet apart from the sound of the waves lapping against the sides of the boat.

You gently drift along the sparkling waters. Stay relaxed as your boat takes you to where you want to go next for your adventure.

Where would you like to go to next?

To go to the MAGICAL MOUNTAIN, turn to page 45
To go to the LAKE OF ENCHANTMENT, turn to page 47
To go to the WOODS OF MYSTERY, turn to page 49
To visit the SECRET GARDEN, turn to page 51
To visit the SHIMMERING SEA, turn to page 53
To go to the WHISPERING GRASSLAND, turn to page 55
To visit the UNKNOWN WILDERNESS, turn to page 57
To visit the RAINBOW WATERFALL, turn to page 59
To go to the SLEEPY STREAMS, turn to page 61
To go to the ANCIENT ISLAND, turn to page 63

Step onto your **HOVER BOARD**

START HERE

Feel yourself using your muscles to balance as the board starts to rise gently into the air. You feel the soft warm air on your face. You can feel the wind in your hair and passing over your whole body. You feel very light and free as you hover through the air.

Notice the landscape as you fly past. The Hover board zooms through the air and you have to keep your balance.

You are light and free

The Hover Board will take you to wherever you wish to go next on your magical adventure.

Where would you like to go? The choice is yours.

To go to the MAGICAL MOUNTAIN, turn to page 45
To go to the LAKE OF ENCHANTMENT, turn to page 47
To go to the WOODS OF MYSTERY, turn to page 49
To visit the SECRET GARDEN, turn to page 51
To visit the SHIMMERING SEA, turn to page 53
To go to the WHISPERING GRASSLAND, turn to page 55
To visit the UNKNOWN WILDERNESS, turn to page 57
To visit the RAINBOW WATERFALL, turn to page 59
To go to the SLEEPY STREAMS, turn to page 61
To go to the ANCIENT ISLAND, turn to page 63

Pick up your MAGIC BROOMSTICK and climb on board

Grasp tightly onto the
broomstick and let the wind
take you up into the air.
Let your legs hang freely as they
dangle from the broomstick.
Allow your whole body to totally relax.
Let your feet relax as they sway gently.
As your feet are hanging downwards,
let all the tension melt away in your legs
as you enjoy this feeling of floating in the
air. Let your arms and shoulders relax.
Enjoy the wind brushing against your face,
relaxing your eyes, your ears, your
forehead, your cheeks and your mouth.

START HERE

You feel as free as a bird

Don't worry or think about anything else but enjoy this experience of flying. Inside you feel so confident; the more confident you feel, the higher you can fly. Sometimes the wind changes direction and you start to pick up speed and fly faster.
It feels so exhilarating to be rushing and swooshing through the air. Other times the wind drops and turns to a light breeze allowing you to float gently. It feels like you are drifting on air.

Keep flying in the air for as long as you wish. When you are ready, let the broomstick take you to the next part of your adventure.

Where are you going next? Where would you like to go?

To go to the MAGICAL MOUNTAIN, turn to page 45
To go to the LAKE OF ENCHANTMENT, turn to page 47
To go to the WOODS OF MYSTERY, turn to page 49
To visit the SECRET GARDEN, turn to page 51
To visit the SHIMMERING SEA, turn to page 53
To go to the WHISPERING GRASSLAND, turn to page 55
To visit the UNKNOWN WILDERNESS, turn to page 57
To visit the RAINBOW WATERFALL, turn to page 59
To go to the SLEEPY STREAMS, turn to page 61
To go to the ANCIENT ISLAND, turn to page 63

Step up into your **ROCKET**. Sit down and fasten your seat belt.

START HERE

Where would you like to go next?
The choice is yours.

To go to the MAGICAL MOUNTAIN, turn to page 45
To go to the LAKE OF ENCHANTMENT, turn to page 47
To go to the WOODS OF MYSTERY, turn to page 49
To visit the SECRET GARDEN, turn to page 51
To visit the SHIMMERING SEA, turn to page 53
To go to the WHISPERING GRASSLAND, turn to page 55
To visit the UNKNOWN WILDERNESS, turn to page 57
To visit the RAINBOW WATERFALL, turn to page 59
To go to the SLEEPY STREAMS, turn to page 61
To go to the ANCIENT ISLAND, turn to page 63

You are about to take the fastest ride of your life. Look at the different colored switches and knobs flashing in front of you. You feel excited at the thought of traveling so fast through the air.

10,9,8,7,6,5,4,3,21
blast off! Off you go speeding into the air.

Off you go speeding into the air. You feel the rocket shake as you blast through the air. Looking through the windows, you see clouds as you rush past. You notice that instead of going into outer space, the rocket makes a curved shape and starts to begin its descent back to Earth.

There are ten buttons on the rocket and you can choose which button you would like to press to take you to the next destination on your magical adventure.

START HERE

You have arrived at your destination.

As you walk down the other side of the mountain, you notice there are different colored doors hidden in the rock. Each one will take you to the next step of your magical adventure.

At this point of the adventure, you can choose to go back through the portal and back to your room or you can choose to carry on with your magical adventure. If you choose to go back, take in a deep breath and breathe out slowly and feel yourself going back through the portal and back to your room. **To exit through the portal turn to page 186**

If you choose to take the next step of your magical adventure, it is time to choose a colored **door**.

Which door would you like to choose?

To go through the RED DOOR, turn to page 65
To go through the BLUE DOOR, turn to page 67
To go through the GREEN DOOR, turn to page 69
To go through the PINK DOOR, turn to page 71
To go through the STONE DOOR, turn to page 73
To go through the ORANGE DOOR, turn to page 75
To go through the GOLDEN DOOR, turn to page 77
To go through the WHITE DOOR, turn to page 79
To go through the SILVER DOOR, turn to page 81
To go through the RAINBOW DOOR, turn to page 83

You have arrived at the **MAGICAL MOUNTAIN**

You start to climb the mountain, step by step by step. It is very steep and seems to reach the clouds. Keep going until you reach the top. It is very windy at the summit. The air is so fresh. You feel so far away from everything here.

From the top of this mountain you can see the entire world. It feels so quiet and peaceful on the top of your mountain. All you hear is the wind blowing past your ears. Feel the cool wind on your face. Take a few moments to enjoy the fresh air.

Breathe in and fill your lungs with this clean mountain air. You can feel your nostrils tingling as you inhale. It feels wonderful to be breathing in such freshness. Relax here for a while and stop your adventure and rest, before moving on to the next step.

You have arrived at the most beautiful

LAKE OF ENCHANTMENT.

Spin around slowly and take in the view. It is truly breathtaking.
All you can see for miles is blue sky and blue water.
You feel your body instantly relax as you look at the sight.
Look at the lake and notice how the gentle breeze causes soft ripples.
The water glitters in the sunlight. The Sun's rays are dancing on the rippling water. As you watch the rippling water, notice how you feel inside.
Notice how you are becoming softer and quieter inside.
You are becoming calm and still like a lake.

You feel calm and quiet

You feel soft and still. You imagine that your mind is like the lake.
On the surface there is some movement, but deep down, there is stillness
and peace. Can you touch the peace and calm inside?
Spend some time walking around the lake feeling still and calm inside.
You notice that all around the lake are different colored doors.
Each one will take you to the next part of your magical adventure.

At this point of the adventure, you can choose to go back
through the portal and back to your room or you can choose
to carry on with your magical adventure. If you choose to
go back, take in a deep breath and breathe out slowly and
feel yourself going back through the portal and back to your
room. **To exit through the portal turn to page 186**

**If you choose to take the next step of your magical
adventure, it is time to choose a colored door.**

Which door would you like to choose?

To go through the RED DOOR, turn to page 65
To go through the BLUE DOOR, turn to page 67
To go through the GREEN DOOR, turn to page 69
To go through the PINK DOOR, turn to page 71
To go through the STONE DOOR, turn to page 73
To go through the ORANGE DOOR, turn to page 75
To go through the GOLDEN DOOR, turn to page 77
To go through the WHITE DOOR, turn to page 79
To go through the SILVER DOOR, turn to page 81
To go through the RAINBOW DOOR, turn to page 83

You have arrived at the

WOODS OF MYSTERY.

Spend some time investigating the wood.
You feel calm and peaceful surrounded by ancient trees.
Take in a deep breath and breathe out slowly.
You can smell the fresh smell of pine needles and earth as
you take each step. Listen to the sounds of twigs
snapping under your feet as you walk. Stop for a moment
and look around.

Which door would you like to choose?

To go through the RED DOOR, turn to page 65
To go through the BLUE DOOR, turn to page 67
To go through the GREEN DOOR, turn to page 69
To go through the PINK DOOR, turn to page 71
To go through the STONE DOOR, turn to page 73
To go through the ORANGE DOOR, turn to page 75
To go through the GOLDEN DOOR, turn to page 77
To go through the WHITE DOOR, turn to page 79
To go through the SILVER DOOR, turn to page 81
To go through the RAINBOW DOOR, turn to page 83

Notice the sounds in the wood.
What can you hear?
Can you hear sounds in the distance?
Can you hear sounds above you in the trees?
Can you hear sounds below you in the undergrowth?

You notice in each large tree
there is a door.
Each door will take you
to the next part of your
magical adventure.

At this point of the adventure, you can choose to go back
through the portal and back to your room or you can choose
to carry on with your magical adventure.
If you choose to go back, take in a deep breath and breathe
out slowly and feel yourself going back through the portal
and back to your room.

To exit through the portal turn to page 186

If you choose to take the next step of your magical
adventure, it is time to choose a colored door.

START HERE

You are now in the SECRET GARDEN

Look around the beautiful garden and notice the sights around you. Notice the sounds of the birds. The Sun is shining, making the colors in the grass and flowers look bright and vibrant.

You are surrounded by flowers and herbs. The breeze is blowing gently and the flowers move delicately. It is almost as if they are dancing.

Spend a few moments feeling relaxed and peaceful as you enjoy the sunshine and look at the colors. You feel so calm and serene.

Feel the breeze on your face as you breathe in. You notice lots of beautiful scents coming from the flowers, fruits and herbs.

Feel the warm air on your skin. Walk past the lavender and take in a deep breath. The scent wafts through your nose and it helps you feel relaxed and calm. You notice a lemon tree and smell one of the lemons.

Its zingy zesty scent fills your nose and head. It helps lift your mood and helps you feel happier.

Pick some of the mint and smell it. Breathe in the the minty smell. It helps you feel even more energetic and refreshes your whole body. Stand in the garden and enjoy the scent of all the aromas. Suddenly, you see all around the garden are different colored doors. Each door will take you to the next step of your magical adventure.

At this point of the adventure, you can choose to go back through the portal and back to your room or you can choose to carry on with your magical adventure. If you choose to go back, take in a deep breath and breathe out slowly and feel yourself going back through the portal and back to your room. **To exit through the portal turn to page 186**

If you choose to take the next step of your magical adventure, it is time to choose a colored door.

Which door would you like to choose?

To go through the RED DOOR, turn to page 65
To go through the BLUE DOOR, turn to page 67
To go through the GREEN DOOR, turn to page 69
To go through the PINK DOOR, turn to page 71
To go through the STONE DOOR, turn to page 73
To go through the ORANGE DOOR, turn to page 75
To go through the GOLDEN DOOR, turn to page 77
To go through the WHITE DOOR, turn to page 79
To go through the SILVER DOOR, turn to page 81
To go through the RAINBOW DOOR, turn to page 83

START HERE

You are now at the

SHIMMERING SEA

Listen to the gentle sound of waves lapping against the shore.
Look at the crystal turquoise blue water.
Spend a few moments watching the waves moving over the sand.
Watch the rhythmic movement of the waves.
Feel your tension melting away as you watch the waves move over the sand. Notice how the sunlight sparkles on the water.
Watch the sparkling water as it ripples gently.
Smell the refreshing ocean salt in the air.
Take in a deep breath and breathe out gently. Breathe in, breathe out. Feel yourself becoming more calm and focused as you breathe in and out.

Enjoy the smell of salt air

Feel the warm Sun on your shoulders and feel the warm breeze on your face and hair. Feel the sand between your fingers and toes. Just relax and breathe. You feel calm and quiet and in control. You walk along by the sea shore and come across some colored doors. Each door will take you to the next part of your magical adventure.

At this point of the adventure, you can choose to go back through the portal and back to your room or you can choose to carry on with your magical adventure. If you choose to go back, take in a deep breath and breathe out slowly and feel yourself going back through the portal and back to your room. **To exit through the portal turn to page 186.**

If you choose to take the next step of your magical adventure, it is time to choose a colored door.

Which door would you like to choose?

To go through the RED DOOR, turn to page 65
To go through the BLUE DOOR, turn to page 67
To go through the GREEN DOOR, turn to page 69
To go through the PINK DOOR, turn to page 71
To go through the STONE DOOR, turn to page 73
To go through the ORANGE DOOR, turn to page 75
To go through the GOLDEN DOOR, turn to page 77
To go through the WHITE DOOR, turn to page 79
To go through the SILVER DOOR, turn to page 81
To go through the RAINBOW DOOR, turn to page 83

START HERE

You are now at the WHISPERING GRASSLAND

Stand in the middle of the tall grasses and watch as the wind moves over each one.
Watch the grass sway gently in the breeze.
As you stand there, imagine you are like the long grass. Fix your feet firmly to the ground and feel the wind gently blowing all over you. You are swaying from side to side and forward and back. Your whole body is totally relaxed and free. All your worries have drifted away. You feel calm and relaxed as you stand there swaying in the breeze.

When you are ready, walk across the grassland and you come across some colored doors. Each door will take you to the next part of your magical adventure.

At this point of the adventure, you can choose to go back through the portal and back to your room or you can choose to carry on with your magical adventure. If you choose to go back, take in a deep breath and breathe out slowly and feel yourself going back through the portal and back to your room. **To exit through the portal turn to page 186**

If you choose to take the next step of your magical adventure, it is time to choose a colored door.

Which door would you like to choose?

To go through the RED DOOR, turn to page 65
To go through the BLUE DOOR, turn to page 67
To go through the GREEN DOOR, turn to page 69
To go through the PINK DOOR, turn to page 71
To go through the STONE DOOR, turn to page 73
To go through the ORANGE DOOR, turn to page 75
To go through the GOLDEN DOOR, turn to page 77
To go through the WHITE DOOR, turn to page 79
To go through the SILVER DOOR, turn to page 81
To go through the RAINBOW DOOR, turn to page 83

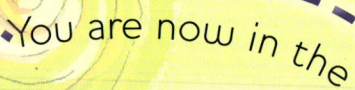

START HERE

You are now in the

UNKOWN WILDERNESS

It is very quiet apart from the sounds of animals in the distance. Stay still and listen to the sounds of the jungle. You can hear all sorts of animal chatting, squawking, roaring and snorting. The jungle is quite a noisy place. Look around and see all the different shades of green in the wilderness. This is a rich place, filled with color and activity, energy and vibrance. There is always something new to hear and something new to see each moment. The more still you can be, the more you can enjoy the sights and sounds of the jungle. Continue to breathe in and out, enjoying watching and listening to the sounds of the jungle.

Right in the middle of the wilderness, you see the oddest thing. You notice a set of different colored doors. Each door will take you to the next part of your magical adventure.

At this point of the adventure, you can choose to go back through the portal and back to your room or you can choose to carry on with your magical adventure. If you choose to go back, take in a deep breath and breathe out slowly and feel yourself going back through the portal and back to your room. **To exit through the portal turn to page 186**

If you choose to take the next step of your magical adventure, it is time to choose a colored door.

Which door would you like to choose?

To go through the RED DOOR, turn to page 65
To go through the BLUE DOOR, turn to page 67
To go through the GREEN DOOR, turn to page 69
To go through the PINK DOOR, turn to page 71
To go through the STONE DOOR, turn to page 73
To go through the ORANGE DOOR, turn to page 75
To go through the GOLDEN DOOR, turn to page 77
To go through the WHITE DOOR, turn to page 79
To go through the SILVER DOOR, turn to page 81
To go through the RAINBOW DOOR, turn to page 83

You are standing by the most beautiful

RAINBOW WATERFALL

The gushing water is glistening in the sunshine. You feel the warmth of the sunshine on your face and body. Go up to the water and step into the wonderful waterfall. The waterfall takes away all your stress, anxiety, worry, and all your angry and frustrated thoughts and feelings. Stand under the powerful waterfall and feel the pure water gushing over your whole body. It feels cleansing and clearing.

As you stand under the water, you feel as though all your negative emotions are flowing away with the water. The water carries them all away. Feel the thoughts of upset and anxiety melting away from your head as the water washes over you. Feel everything melting away.

Behind the powerful waterfall, you notice a row of different colored doors. Each door will take you to the next part of your magical adventure.

At this point of the adventure, you can choose to go back through the portal and back to your room or you can choose to carry on with your magical adventure. If you choose to go back, take in a deep breath and breathe out slowly and feel yourself going back through the portal and back to your room. **To exit through the portal turn to page 186**

If you choose to take the next step of your magical adventure, it is time to choose a colored door.

Which door would you like to choose?

To go through the **RED DOOR,** turn to page **65**
To go through the **BLUE DOOR,** turn to page **67**
To go through the **GREEN DOOR,** turn to page **69**
To go through the **PINK DOOR,** turn to page **71**
To go through the **STONE DOOR,** turn to page **73**
To go through the **ORANGE DOOR,** turn to page **75**
To go through the **GOLDEN DOOR,** turn to page **77**
To go through the **WHITE DOOR,** turn to page **79**
To go through the **SILVER DOOR,** turn to page **81**
To go through the **RAINBOW DOOR,** turn to page **83**

START HERE

You find yourself by the

SLEEPY STREAM

Everything is so calm here. You feel relaxed just by being here.
Take a moment to lie down next to the gentle stream.
Allow your body to relax as you feel the warm Sun on your body.
You can hear the gentle ripples of the water. Feel your feet
relaxing. Let your toes completely relax and become soft.
Let this feeling spread gently through your feet. Now squeeze your
legs and gently let them go. Feel all the tension in your legs being
released as they become relaxed and soft. Let your tummy and back
relax. Let your neck become soft. Feel all the tension melting away.
Relax your arms and relax your head. Stay there for a few more
moments, enjoying the feeling of being completely relaxed as
you listen to the gentle trickle of the stream.

To go through the RED DOOR, turn to page 65
To go through the BLUE DOOR, turn to page 67
To go through the GREEN DOOR, turn to page 69
To go through the PINK DOOR, turn to page 71
To go through the STONE DOOR, turn to page 73
To go through the ORANGE DOOR, turn to page 75
To go through the GOLDEN DOOR, turn to page 77
To go through the WHITE DOOR, turn to page 79
To go through the SILVER DOOR, turn to page 81
To go through the RAINBOW DOOR, turn to page 83

By the side of the sleepy streams are different colored doors. Each door will take you to the next part of your magical adventure.

At this point of the adventure, you can choose to go back through the portal and back to your room or you can choose to carry on with your magical adventure. If you choose to go back, take in a deep breath and breathe out slowly and feel yourself going back through the portal and back to your room. **To exit through the portal turn to page 186**

If you choose to take the next step of your magical adventure, it is time to choose a colored door.

Which door would you like to choose?

You are now on an

ANCIENT ISLAND

START HERE

Feel the warmth of the Sun on your body as you sit on the warm earth. As you sit there, you become absorbed by the beauty around you. You notice the palm trees, gently swaying in the breeze. You focus on the colorful birds and wildlife. You feel soft and quiet inside as you enjoy sitting on your own ancient island.

As you sit here, take in a deep breath and breathe out as slowly as you can. Breathe in, breathe out.

Take a walk around the ancient island and you notice something strange. Scattered around this ancient island are different colored doors. Each door will take you to the next part of your magical adventure.

At this point of the adventure, you can choose to go back through the portal and back to your room or you can choose to carry on with your magical adventure. If you choose to go back, take in a deep breath and breathe out slowly and feel yourself going back through the portal and back to your room. **To exit through the portal turn to page 186**

If you choose to take the next step of your magical adventure, it is time to choose a colored door.

To go through the **RED DOOR**, turn to page 65
To go through the **BLUE DOOR**, turn to page 67
To go through the **GREEN DOOR**, turn to page 69
To go through the **PINK DOOR**, turn to page 71
To go through the **STONE DOOR**, turn to page 73
To go through the **ORANGE DOOR**, turn to page 75
To go through the **GOLDEN DOOR**, turn to page 77
To go through the **WHITE DOOR**, turn to page 79
To go through the **SILVER DOOR**, turn to page 81
To go through the **RAINBOW DOOR**, turn to page 83

Step through the Red Door...

and you find a pathway made of red bricks. Walk along as slowly as you can, putting one foot in front of the other, mindfully. Become aware of how hard or soft the path is under your feet. Take each step with care.

As you step, notice where the sounds are coming from.
What can you hear to your right? What can you hear to your left?
What can you hear in front of you? What can you hear behind you?
What can you hear above you? What can you hear below you?
Notice all the sounds around you. Notice if they are nearby or in the distance. Notice how loud or soft the sounds are.
Be aware of how high or low the sounds are.
Spend some time listening to all the sounds around you.

Repeat to yourself "I am aware of the sounds around me.

"I am aware of the sounds around me."

At the end of the red brick pathway, you stop. You have come to a signpost. It is time for you to choose where you are going next. You can either go back through the portal or you can go on for the next part of the magical adventure. If you choose to go back through the portal, take in a deep breath and breathe out slowly three times as you feel yourself coming back from your magical world, through the portal and back to the room.

To exit through the portal turn to page 186

Cave of Calm   Maze of Miracles

Palace of Peace   Room of Rest

Castle of Creativity   Hut of Happiness

House of Hearts

Den of Dreams   Tower of Power

Well of Wishes

If you choose to continue your adventure, choose one of the destinations on the signpost:

To go to the **CAVE of CALM, turn to page 85**
To go to the **HUT OF HAPPINESS, turn to page 87**
To go to the **DEN OF DREAMS, turn to page 89**
To go to the **HOUSE OF HEARTS, turn to page 91**
To go to the **TOWER OF POWER, turn to page 93**
To go to the **WELL OF WISHES, turn to page 95**
To go to the **CASTLE OF CREATIVITY, turn to page 97**
To go to the **ROOM OF REST, turn to page 99**
To go to the **MAZE OF MIRACLES, turn to page 101**
To go to the **PALACE OF PEACE, turn to page 103**

Step through the **Blue Door**

and you find a pathway made of soft fluffy clouds. Walk along as slowly as you can, putting one foot in front of the other, mindfully. As you step, your whole body feels like a soft cloud. You feel so light.

Each time you have a thought, you create a little thought bubble, like a cloud above your head. Spend some time noticing what thought bubbles you have floating above you. Are they happy and peaceful thought bubbles that gently bounce above you? Or are they noisy, angry thought bubbles that shoot through the air? Your thought bubbles float through the air and affect other people. You can choose what type of thought bubbles you would like to send through the air.

Spend some time creating happy and peaceful thought bubbles. Fill your bubbles with happy thoughts and send them through the air to others.

Repeat to yourself "I am happy and peaceful,

"I am happy and peaceful,"

At the end of the blue cloud pathway, you stop. You have come to a signpost. It is time for you to choose where you are going next. You can either go back through the portal or you can go on for the next part of the magical adventure.

If you choose to go back through the portal, take in a deep breath and breathe out slowly three times as you feel yourself coming back from your magical world, through the portal and back to the room.

To exit through the portal turn to page 186

Cave of Calm   *Maze of Miracles*

Palace of Peace   *Room of Rest*

Castle of Creativity   *Hut of Happiness*

House of Hearts

Den of Dreams   *Tower of Power*

Well of Wishes

If you choose to continue your adventure, choose one of the destinations on the signpost:

To go to the CAVE of CALM, turn to page 85
To go to the HUT OF HAPPINESS, turn to page 87
To go to the DEN OF DREAMS, turn to page 89
To go to the HOUSE OF HEARTS, turn to page 91
To go to the TOWER OF POWER, turn to page 93
To go to the WELL OF WISHES, turn to page 95
To go to the CASTLE OF CREATIVITY, turn to page 97
To go to the ROOM OF REST, turn to page 99
To go to the MAZE OF MIRACLES, turn to page 101
To go to the PALACE OF PEACE, turn to page 103

START HERE

Step through the Green Door

and you find a grassy path. Walk along as slowly as you can, putting one foot in front of the other, mindfully. Feel the soft grass underneath your feet and between your toes. Take each step with care.

As you walk, imagine you have special mindful glasses on. When you look through your mindful glasses, you see everything clearly. The colors are brighter and the shapes are sharper. You can see every tiny detail. Wearing your mindful glasses helps you become very mindful and aware of what is going on around you. What do you see? Notice all the shapes and the textures of what you see through your mindful glasses. Notice the patterns. Notice the colors. Become very aware of what is around you as you continue to walk along

Repeat to yourself "I am mindful, I am mindful."

At the end of the grassy path, you stop. You have come to a signpost. It is time for you to choose where you are going next. You can either go back through the portal or you can go on for the next part of the magical adventure. If you choose to go back through the portal, take in a deep breath and breathe out slowly three times as you feel yourself coming back from your magical world, through the portal and back to the room.

To exit through the portal turn to page 186

If you choose to continue your adventure, choose one of the destinations on the signpost:

Cave of Calm — Maze of Miracles
Palace of Peace — Room of Rest
Castle of Creativity — Hut of Happiness
House of Hearts
Den of Dreams — Tower of Power
Well of Wishes

To go to the **CAVE of CALM,** turn to page 85
To go to the **HUT OF HAPPINESS,** turn to page 87
To go to the **DEN OF DREAMS,** turn to page 89
To go to the **HOUSE OF HEARTS,** turn to page 91
To go to the **TOWER OF POWER,** turn to page 93
To go to the **WELL OF WISHES,** turn to page 95
To go to the **CASTLE OF CREATIVITY,** turn to page 97
To go to the **ROOM OF REST,** turn to page 99
To go to the **MAZE OF MIRACLES,** turn to page 101
To go to the **PALACE OF PEACE,** turn to page 103

Step through the Pink Door

and you find a path of soft marshmallows. Walk along as slowly as you can, putting one foot in front of the other, mindfully. Feel the soft marshmallows under your feet. Take each step with care.

As you walk, imagine your whole body is becoming soft like a marshmallow. Take in a deep breath and feel yourself becoming soft and light. Become aware of your fingers. Become aware of your whole body. Your body feels soft and light. Bring your awareness to your breathing. Take in a deep breath and as you breathe out, feel yourself getting lighter and lighter. How light can you be? You enjoy feeling light and free.

Repeat to yourself, "I am soft, I am soft."

At the end of the marshmallow pathway, you stop. You have come to a signpost. It is time for you to choose where you are going next. You can either go back through the portal or you can go on for the next part of the magical adventure. If you choose to go back through the portal, take in a deep breath and breathe out slowly three times as you feel yourself coming back from your magical world, through the portal and back to the room.

To exit through the portal turn to page 186

If you choose to continue your adventure, choose one of the destinations on the signpost:

To go to the **CAVE of CALM, turn to page 85**
To go to the **HUT OF HAPPINESS, turn to page 87**
To go to the **DEN OF DREAMS, turn to page 89**
To go to the **HOUSE OF HEARTS, turn to page 91**
To go to the **TOWER OF POWER, turn to page 93**
To go to the **WELL OF WISHES, turn to page 95**
To go to the **CASTLE OF CREATIVITY, turn to page 97**
To go to the **ROOM OF REST, turn to page 99**
To go to the **MAZE OF MIRACLES, turn to page 101**
To go to the **PALACE OF PEACE, turn to page 103**

Step through the Stone Door

and you find a pebbly path. Walk along as slowly as you can, putting one foot in front of the other, mindfully. Become aware of how hard or soft the path is under your feet. Take each step with care.

Stop and pick up a pebble from the path. Hold the pebble in your hand and close your eyes. Breathe in and out deeply as you hold the pebble. Focus on the pebble in your hand and become completely aware of the pebble and nothing else. Breathe in and breathe out slowly as you feel the pebble in your hand. How cool is the pebble? How smooth is the pebble? What shape is the pebble?
See if you can be as still and silent as the pebble.
Continue to hold the pebble, becoming still and silent.

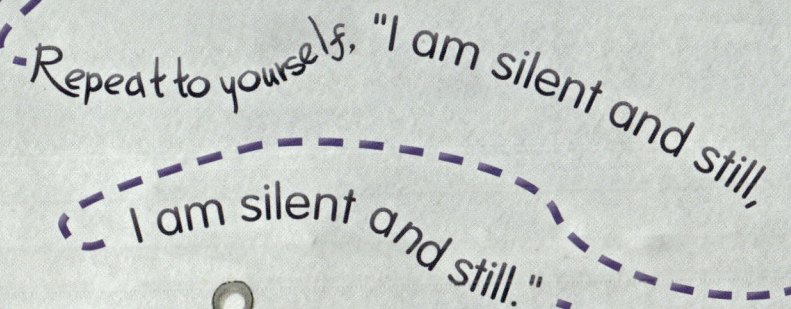

Repeat to yourself, "I am silent and still,

I am silent and still."

At the end of the pebbly pathway, you stop. You have come to a signpost. It is time for you to choose where you are going next. You can either go back through the portal or you can go on for the next part of the magical adventure. If you choose to go back through the portal, take in a deep breath and breathe out slowly three times as you feel yourself coming back from your magical world, through the portal and back to the room.

To exit through the portal turn to page 186

If you choose to continue your adventure, choose one of the destinations on the signpost:

To go to the CAVE of CALM, turn to page 85
To go to the HUT OF HAPPINESS, turn to page 87
To go to the DEN OF DREAMS, turn to page 89
To go to the HOUSE OF HEARTS, turn to page 91
To go to the TOWER OF POWER, turn to page 93
To go to the WELL OF WISHES, turn to page 95
To go to the CASTLE OF CREATIVITY, turn to page 97
To go to the ROOM OF REST, turn to page 99
To go to the MAZE OF MIRACLES, turn to page 101
To go to the PALACE OF PEACE, turn to page 103

START HERE

Step through the Orange Door

and you find a beautiful, leafy pathway.
Walk along as slowly as you can, putting one foot in front of the other,
mindfully. Become aware of the soft leaves under your feet.
Take each step with care.

As you walk along the soft, scrunchy path, imagine your eyes are
windows. When your eyes are closed, the room inside your head is dark.
It is as though the curtains are drawn and the light is shut out.
You can feel safe and peaceful in your room. Do you notice how you feel
now you have drawn your curtains? Now, open your curtains very slowly.
Open your eyes and look out of your windows. Gently look around.
What do you see through your windows? What can you see outside your
room? Notice the colors of the leaves all around you.
Continue to walk along the path as you stay still and quiet in the room
in your head, looking out of your windows.

Repeat to yourself, "I am calm, I am calm."

At the end of the leafy path, you stop. You have come to a signpost. It is time for you to choose where you are going next. You can either go back through the portal or you can go on for the next part of the magical adventure.

If you choose to go back through the portal, take in a deep breath and breathe out slowly three times as you feel yourself coming back from your magical world, through the portal and back to the room.

To exit through the portal turn to page 186

If you choose to continue your adventure, choose one of the destinations on the signpost:

Cave of Calm · Maze of Miracles
Palace of Peace · Room of Rest
Castle of Creativity · Hut of Happiness · House of Hearts
Den of Dreams · Tower of Power
Well of Wishes

To go to the CAVE of CALM, turn to page 85
To go to the HUT OF HAPPINESS, turn to page 87
To go to the DEN OF DREAMS, turn to page 89
To go to the HOUSE OF HEARTS, turn to page 91
To go to the TOWER OF POWER, turn to page 93
To go to the WELL OF WISHES, turn to page 95
To go to the CASTLE OF CREATIVITY, turn to page 97
To go to the ROOM OF REST, turn to page 99
To go to the MAZE OF MIRACLES, turn to page 101
To go to the PALACE OF PEACE, turn to page 103

START HERE

Step through the

Golden Door

and you find a path of gold. Walk along as slowly as you can, putting one foot in front of the other, mindfully.

As you walk along the golden path, something magical happens. With each step you feel as if your whole body is turning into golden light. Take your first step and feel your right leg turning to a beautiful golden light, take the next step and feel your left leg turning into golden light. Next feel your chest and stomach turning to light. With the next steps, you feel your arms turning into light. Finally you feel your neck and head transforming into a beautiful golden light.

Your whole body is made of light. Light is running through your veins. Light is in every single cell. It feels so wonderful to have a body of light. Spend a few moments enjoying your body of light.

Repeat to yourself, "I am light, I am light."

At the end of the golden path, you stop. You have come to a signpost. It is time for you to choose where you are going next. You can either go back through the portal or you can go on for the next part of the magical adventure. If you choose to go back through the portal, take in a deep breath and breathe out slowly three times as you feel yourself coming back from your magical world, through the portal and back to the room.

To exit through the portal turn to page 186

If you choose to continue your adventure, choose one of the destinations on the signpost:

To go to the CAVE of CALM, turn to page 85
To go to the HUT OF HAPPINESS, turn to page 87
To go to the DEN OF DREAMS, turn to page 89
To go to the HOUSE OF HEARTS, turn to page 91
To go to the TOWER OF POWER, turn to page 93
To go to the WELL OF WISHES, turn to page 95
To go to the CASTLE OF CREATIVITY, turn to page 97
To go to the ROOM OF REST, turn to page 99
To go to the MAZE OF MIRACLES, turn to page 101
To go to the PALACE OF PEACE, turn to page 103

Step through the White Door

and you find a path of crisp, white snow. Walk along as slowly as you can, putting one foot in front of the other, mindfully. Become aware of how soft the snow is under your feet. Notice how the snow crunches with every step. Take each step with care.

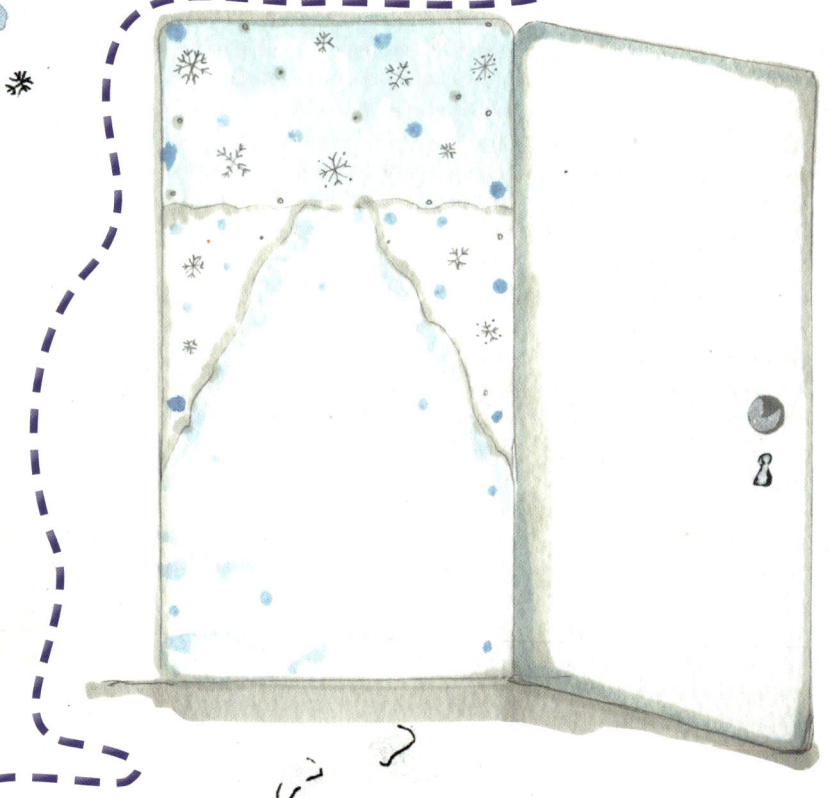

As you walk, notice the snowflakes falling gently from the sky. For a moment, think about your mind. All your thoughts are floating through your mind like snowflakes in a snow globe. You can help all the scattered thoughts become quiet. Stay still and take in a deep breath. As you breathe out, let all the thoughts gently settle. Breathe in, breathe out, breathe in, breathe out. As you breathe, notice how the thoughts are gently settling down in your head. Watch how the thoughts are gently calming down and coming to rest. You start to feel calm and quiet.

Repeat to yourself, "I am quiet and calm, I am quiet and calm."

At the end of the snowy pathway, you stop. You have come to a signpost. It is time for you to choose where you are going next. You can either go back through the portal or you can go on for the next part of the magical adventure. If you choose to go back through the portal, take in a deep breath and breathe out slowly three times as you feel yourself coming back from your magical world, through the portal and back to the room.

To exit through the portal turn to page 186

Cave of Calm
Maze of Miracles
Palace of Peace
Room of Rest
Castle of Creativity
Hut of Happiness
House of Hearts
Den of Dreams
Tower of Power
Well of Wishes

If you choose to continue your adventure, choose one of the destinations on the signpost:

To go to the CAVE of CALM, turn to page 85
To go to the HUT OF HAPPINESS, turn to page 87
To go to the DEN OF DREAMS, turn to page 89
To go to the HOUSE OF HEARTS, turn to page 91
To go to the TOWER OF POWER, turn to page 93
To go to the WELL OF WISHES, turn to page 95
To go to the CASTLE OF CREATIVITY, turn to page 97
To go to the ROOM OF REST, turn to page 99
To go to the MAZE OF MIRACLES, turn to page 101
To go to the PALACE OF PEACE, turn to page 103

START HERE

Step through the Silver Door

and you find a tunnel of sparkling morning mist. Walk through the beautiful tunnel of mist. Feel the mist swirling around you as you place one foot in front of another.

Notice how your body feels as you walk through the sparkling mist. How do you feel? Breathe in, breathe out. Notice how the mist feels on your skin. Breathe in, breathe out. Notice the mist all around you. Breathe in, breathe out. Notice how soft your body feels as you step through the misty tunnel. Breathe in, breathe out. You start to feel soft inside. Breathe in, breathe out. You start to feel relaxed. Notice what thoughts are in your head as you step through the tunnel. Be aware of what is going on outside your body and what is happening inside.

Repeat to yourself, "I am aware of my breath

I am aware of my body."

At the end of the sparkling misty tunnel, you stop. You have come to a signpost. It is time for you to choose where you are going next. You can either go back through the portal or you can go on for the next part of the magical adventure. If you choose to go back through the portal, take in a deep breath and breathe out slowly three times as you feel yourself coming back from your magical world, through the portal and back to the room.

Cave of Calm
Maze of Miracles
Palace of Peace
Room of Rest
Castle of Creativity
Hut of Happiness
House of Hearts
Den of Dreams
Well of Wishes
Tower of Power

To exit through the portal turn to page 186

If you choose to continue your adventure, choose one of the destinations on the signpost:

To go to the CAVE of CALM, turn to page 85
To go to the HUT OF HAPPINESS, turn to page 87
To go to the DEN OF DREAMS, turn to page 89
To go to the HOUSE OF HEARTS, turn to page 91
To go to the TOWER OF POWER, turn to page 93
To go to the WELL OF WISHES, turn to page 95
To go to the CASTLE OF CREATIVITY, turn to page 97
To go to the ROOM OF REST, turn to page 99
To go to the MAZE OF MIRACLES, turn to page 101
To go to the PALACE OF PEACE, turn to page 103

 START HERE

Step through the

Rainbow Door

and you find a rainbow pathway. Walk along as slowly as you can, putting one foot in front of the other, mindfully.

As you walk along the glittering rainbow path, you start to feel more and more happy. Put your hand on your chest and spend a few moments noticing how you feel.
Now, imagine that you have a smile in your heart.
Can you see the smile in your heart?
Watch how you start to have loving feelings.
Can you send that smile up to your face?
Let your mouth smile gently. Feel the smile on your face.
Feel the smile in your eyes.

Repeat to yourself, "I am smiling,

I am smiling."

At the end of the rainbow path, you stop. You have come to a signpost. It is time for you to choose where you are going next. You can either go back through the portal or you can go on for the next part of the magical adventure. If you choose to go back through the portal, take in a deep breath and breathe out slowly three times as you feel yourself coming back from your magical world, through the portal and back to the room.

Cave of Calm   Maze of Miracles

Palace of Peace   Room of Rest

Castle of Creativity   Hut of Happiness

House of Hearts

Den of Dreams

Well of Wishes   Tower of Power

To exit through the portal turn to page 186

If you choose to continue your adventure, choose one of the destinations on the signpost:

To go to the CAVE of CALM, turn to page 85
To go to the HUT OF HAPPINESS, turn to page 87
To go to the DEN OF DREAMS, turn to page 89
To go to the HOUSE OF HEARTS, turn to page 91
To go to the TOWER OF POWER, turn to page 93
To go to the WELL OF WISHES, turn to page 95
To go to the CASTLE OF CREATIVITY, turn to page 97
To go to the ROOM OF REST, turn to page 99
To go to the MAZE OF MIRACLES, turn to page 101
To go to the PALACE OF PEACE, turn to page 103

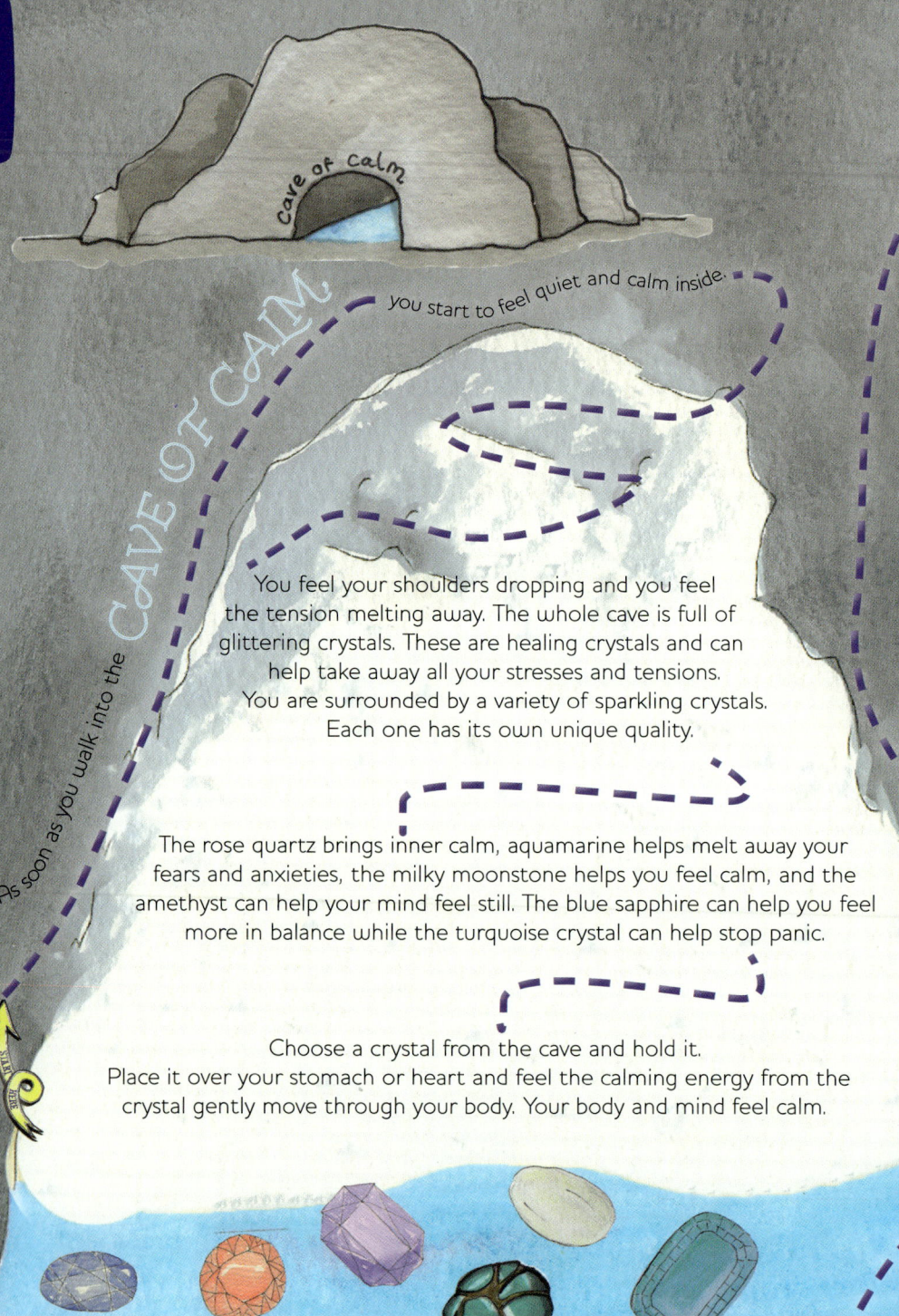

Cave of calm

CAVE OF CALM

As soon as you walk into the

you start to feel quiet and calm inside.

You feel your shoulders dropping and you feel the tension melting away. The whole cave is full of glittering crystals. These are healing crystals and can help take away all your stresses and tensions. You are surrounded by a variety of sparkling crystals. Each one has its own unique quality.

The rose quartz brings inner calm, aquamarine helps melt away your fears and anxieties, the milky moonstone helps you feel calm, and the amethyst can help your mind feel still. The blue sapphire can help you feel more in balance while the turquoise crystal can help stop panic.

Choose a crystal from the cave and hold it. Place it over your stomach or heart and feel the calming energy from the crystal gently move through your body. Your body and mind feel calm.

Go to a corner of the cave. In the shadows, there is someone waiting to meet you. It is now time for you to choose what you are going to do next.
You can either take a step forward to meet your visitor or go back through the portal. If you choose to go back through the portal, take in a deep breath and breathe out slowly three times as you feel yourself coming back from your magical world, through the portal and back to the room.

To exit through the portal turn to page 186

This is what my CAVE OF CALM looks like

Who would you like to meet?

You can draw your Cave of Calm here.

To meet a WISE MAN, turn to page 105
To meet an ANGEL, turn to page 107
To meet a WIZARD, turn to page 109
To meet an ELF, turn to page 111
To meet a FORTUNE TELLER, turn to page 113
To meet a GENIE, turn to page 115
To meet the QUEEN OF HEARTS, turn to page 117
To meet your SPIRIT GUIDE turn to page 119
To meet a GODDESS, turn to page 121
To meet a SUPERHERO, turn to page 123

Step into the **HUT OF HAPPINESS**

The Hut of Happiness holds all your positive and happy memories. On each wall, you see screens. Each screen is showing a happy memory from your past. You see yourself playing, running, being in nature, being with people who are closest to you. All the colors are really bright and you can hear yourself laughing. You can see yourself smiling. It is almost as though you are back in that memory. Now, to make the memory even stronger, turn up the sound and the color on the screen. Everything is louder and brighter. It is like you are back in the situation. You can feel bubbles of happiness in your stomach. Feel the tingling and bubbling sensations in your heart and stomach. Take in a deep breath and breathe in a feeling of happiness. Breathe out. Hold on to this happy feeling as you watch your special memories on the screen. When your memory is at its brightest, gently squeeze your thumb and first finger together. Take in a deep breath, holding the memory as you squeeze your thumb and finger, and breathe out as slowly as you can. Next time that you feel sad, all you have to do is close your eyes and put your thumb and first finger together again and you will remember your happy memory. This is your happiness switch and will bring you back to the Hut of Happiness whenever you wish.

Breathe in happiness, breathe out happiness.

This is what My HUT OF HAPPINESS looks like

You can draw your Hut of Happiness here.

There is a chair in the corner of the hut. Sitting on the chair is someone who would like to meet you. It is now time for you to choose what you are going to do next. You can either take a step forward to meet your visitor or go back through the portal. If you choose to go back through the portal, take in a deep breath and breathe out slowly three times as you feel yourself coming back from your magical world, through the portal and back to the room.

To exit through the portal turn to page 186

Who would you like to meet?

To meet a **WISE MAN**, turn to page 105
To meet an **ANGEL**, turn to page 107
To meet a **WIZARD**, turn to page 109
To meet an **ELF**, turn to page 111
To meet a **FORTUNE TELLER**, turn to page 113
To meet a **GENIE**, turn to page 115
To meet the **QUEEN OF HEARTS**, turn to page 117
To meet your **SPIRIT GUIDE** turn to page 119
To meet a **GODDESS**, turn to page 121
To meet a **SUPERHERO**, turn to page 123

DEN OF DREAMS

Den of Dreams

Walk into your

This is the place where you can make and build your goals and dreams. Once you have built your dreams, you can hang them in dream catchers around the den.

Have a think about all the things that you are good at and see if you can identify your own personal talents and greatness. If you could do whatever you wanted to in the world, what would it be? If no one was stopping you, what would you love to do? If you could go wherever you wanted, where would it be?
Spend some time thinking about what you would love to do.
Imagine yourself doing this in the future. See yourself doing the things you love doing. Now, take a piece of paper and write your dreams down and tie it to one of the dream catchers.

This is what my Den of Dreams looks like

You can draw your Den of Dreams here.

There are hundreds of dream catchers hanging from the ceiling. These dream catchers catch your dreams and hold them safe for you. When you leave the room, you know that your hopes and dreams are kept safe and you can visit again any time, adding to your collection of hopes and dreams. You feel happy knowing that one day all your dreams will come true.

There is someone in your Den of Dreams who would like to meet you.

It is now time for you to choose what you are going to do next. You can either take a step forward to meet your visitor or go back through the portal. If you choose to go back through the portal, take in a deep breath and breathe out slowly three times as you feel yourself coming back from your magical world, through the portal and back to the room.

To exit through the portal turn to page 186

Who would you like to meet?

To meet a WISE MAN, turn to page 105
To meet an ANGEL, turn to page 107
To meet a WIZARD, turn to page 109
To meet an ELF, turn to page 111
To meet a FORTUNE TELLER, turn to page 113
To meet a GENIE, turn to page 115
To meet the QUEEN OF HEARTS, turn to page 117
To meet your SPIRIT GUIDE turn to page 119
To meet a GODDESS, turn to page 121
To meet a SUPERHERO, turn to page 123

Step into the

HOUSE OF HEARTS

This is the most beautiful house, and fills your heart with love and joy as soon as you step inside. You notice on the walls there are hundreds of different sized hearts. There are big hearts, small hearts, and colored ones. They are everywhere. You step closer and notice that the hearts have words on them.
Each heart is a heart of thanks and gratitude and there are all the names of people and things in your life that you are grateful for. Take a look around the gallery of hearts. What is written on the hearts? Who are you grateful for in your life? What do you love? What things in your life are you deeply thankful and grateful for? Spend a few moments reading the hearts and writing on some new ones.

When you have read and written on all the hearts, leave this room and walk next door. There is someone waiting to meet you. It is now time for you to choose what you are going to do next.

This is what my House of Hearts looks like

You can draw your House of Hearts here.

You can either take a step forward to meet your visitor or go back through the portal. If you choose to go back through the portal, take in a deep breath and breathe out slowly three times as you feel yourself coming back from your magical world, through the portal and back to the room.

To exit through the portal turn to page 186

Who would you like to meet?

To meet a **WISE MAN**, turn to page 105
To meet an **ANGEL**, turn to page 107
To meet a **WIZARD**, turn to page 109
To meet an **ELF**, turn to page 111
To meet a **FORTUNE TELLER**, turn to page 113
To meet a **GENIE**, turn to page 115
To meet the **QUEEN OF HEARTS**, turn to page 117
To meet your **SPIRIT GUIDE** turn to page 119
To meet a **GODDESS**, turn to page 121
To meet a **SUPERHERO**, turn to page 123

TOWER OF POWER.

Stand in the middle of the

This is a great place to come to when you feel a little low and small. The Tower of Power is full of strength and power, and a great place for you to build inner strength, resilience and power. It only takes a few moments to build up enough power to last a very long time and help you manage lots of different situations.

How does it feel standing in your Tower of Power?

Take in a deep breath of strength and power, and breathe out strength and power. Breathe in, breathe out. Breathe in strength and power and breathe out strength and power. Fill your Tower of Power with so much power from your mind. Feel yourself surrounded with power. Feel power in every part of your body. Feel strong from the inside. Feel this power in every cell, in every bone, and every organ of your body. Feel courageous and strong. Feel this power in your mind.

You know that when you are breathing your silent power breaths and are inside your power bubble, you are safe. Unkind words and actions from others cannot touch you. When you feel full of power, take the stairs right to the top of the tower.

You can draw your Tower of Power here.

This is what my Tower of Power looks like

There is someone waiting to meet you. It is now time for you to choose what you are going to do next. You can either take a step forward to meet your visitor or go back through the portal. If you choose to go back through the portal, take in a deep breath and breathe out slowly three times as you feel yourself coming back from your magical world, through the portal and back to the room.

Who would you like to meet?

To exit through the portal turn to page 186

To meet a WISE MAN, turn to page 105
To meet an ANGEL, turn to page 107
To meet a WIZARD, turn to page 109
To meet an ELF, turn to page 111
To meet a FORTUNE TELLER, turn to page 113
To meet a GENIE, turn to page 115
To meet the QUEEN OF HEARTS, turn to page 117
To meet your SPIRIT GUIDE turn to page 119
To meet a GODDESS, turn to page 121
To meet a SUPERHERO, turn to page 123

Look into the **WELL OF WISHES**

It is a long way down and you can
see the magical waters below.
What color is the water?
Can you see it sparkling or see any
reflections in the water? Now, spend a few
moments thinking about your life and any
difficulties you might have.
What problems or challenges do you have in your life?
What would you like to change?
What do you wish for? You can make as many wishes as you
like in the Well of Wishes. Stay very still and make a wish.
As you stay there, imagine your wish coming true and think about
how you would feel if it did come true. Just imagine what your life would
be like when your wish come true. Notice every detail. Make the pictures
bright in your mind and the sounds loud. Really feel what it would be like to
have all your wishes come true. How would you feel?

**Imagine the feelings you would have in your body.
Imagine what thoughts you would have. When you are ready, you
can make another wish. Make as many wishes as you want.
When you have made all of your wishes, stay still and take a deep
breath and breathe out slowly.**

This is what my Well of Wishes looks like

You can draw your Well of Wishes here.

It is now time for you to choose what you are going to do next. You can either take a step forward to meet your visitor or go back through the portal. If you choose to go back through the portal, take in a deep breath and breathe out slowly three times as you feel yourself coming back from your magical world, through the portal and back to the room.

To exit through the portal turn to page 186

To meet a WISE MAN, turn to page 105
To meet an ANGEL, turn to page 107
To meet a WIZARD, turn to page 109
To meet an ELF, turn to page 111
To meet a FORTUNE TELLER, turn to page 113
To meet a GENIE, turn to page 115
To meet the QUEEN OF HEARTS, turn to page 117
To meet your SPIRIT GUIDE turn to page 119
To meet a GODDESS, turn to page 121
To meet a SUPERHERO, turn to page 123

Who would you like to meet?

You find yourself in the **CASTLE OF CREATIVITY**

This is a special castle where the inside walls are white. You are free to paint and color all over the walls in whatever creative way you choose.

FREE

Pick up a brush and paints, and choose a section of the wall. Relax your shoulders, take in a deep breath and breathe out as slowly as you can. You are going to give your brain a few minutes rest as you paint the walls. Move your brush around the paper. There is no need to worry about creating a good picture or making sense, just enjoy making shapes and patterns on the paper. Take in a deep breath again and as you breathe out, let your brush move to the out breath. Breathe in and breathe out and let you brush go free. Enjoy the feeling of moving the brush all around the paper. It is like a dance. You feel very wild and free. It feels such fun being able to color any wall in the castle. Slowly, you notice the walls becoming colored in. You know that you can visit the palace at any time.

When you have finished your coloring, you get up and walk to the throne room. You see someone at the end of the long room sitting on a throne.

THIS IS WHAT MY CASTLE OF CREATIVITY LOOKS LIKE

You can draw your Castle of Creativity here

It is now time for you to choose what you are going to do next. You can either take a step forward to meet your visitor or go back through the portal. If you choose to go back through the portal, take in a deep breath and breathe out slowly three times as you feel yourself coming back from your magical world, through the portal and back to the room.

To exit through the portal turn to page 186

Who would you like to meet?

To meet a WISE MAN, turn to page 105
To meet an ANGEL, turn to page 107
To meet a WIZARD, turn to page 109
To meet an ELF, turn to page 111
To meet a FORTUNE TELLER, turn to page 113
To meet a GENIE, turn to page 115
To meet the QUEEN OF HEARTS, turn to page 117
To meet your SPIRIT GUIDE turn to page 119
To meet a GODDESS, turn to page 121
To meet a SUPERHERO, turn to page 123

ROOM OF REST.

Step into the

Everything in here is designed to help you rest and sleep well.
The room is decorated in soft blues and greens to help rest your eyes and
help you feel calm. There is a scent button where you can choose which
calming aromatherapy scent you would like diffused through the air.
You can choose lavender oil for calm and rest, rose oil for
anxiety, mandarin to feel safe and jasmine oil to help you sleep.

On the floor is a pile of the softest cushions. Lie down and get comfortable
on them. You have never felt such softness. The cushions are made of velvet
and so soft to touch. You can stroke the cushions with your hands.
As soon as your face touches the soft velvety cushions, you want to rest
and melt all the way into them. The cushions have a lovely scent that helps
you feel calm and relaxed. You feel so calm and restful.
All the muscles in your head and neck soften, and you feel relaxed.
Your face feels soft and relaxed. Take in a deep breath and feel yourself
sinking deeply into the cushions. You feel more and more relaxed.
Breathe in and relax, breathe out and relax. As you lie softly on the cushions
you feel all your troubles gently floating away, leaving you with a feeling of
peace and calm. You feel peaceful. You feel safe. You feel comfortable.
You feel comforted. You feel quiet. You feel soft.
You feel safe and comforted. You feel quiet and peaceful.
You feel you could just drift off to a dreamy sleep.

Have a rest here for awhile

When you feel rested, stretch your whole body and notice there is someone else in the room with you.

This is what my Room of Rest looks like.

You can draw your Room of Rest here

It is now time for you to choose what you are going to do next. You can either take a step forward to meet your visitor or go back through the portal. If you choose to go back through the portal, take in a deep breath and breathe out slowly three times as you feel yourself coming back from your magical world, through the portal and back to the room.

To exit through the portal turn to page 186

Who would you like to meet?

To meet a **WISE MAN**, turn to page 105
To meet an **ANGEL**, turn to page 107
To meet a **WIZARD**, turn to page 109
To meet an **ELF**, turn to page 111
To meet a **FORTUNE TELLER**, turn to page 113
To meet a **GENIE**, turn to page 115
To meet the **QUEEN OF HEARTS**, turn to page 117
To meet your **SPIRIT GUIDE** turn to page 119
To meet a **GODDESS**, turn to page 121
To meet a **SUPERHERO**, turn to page 123

MAZE OF MIRACLES

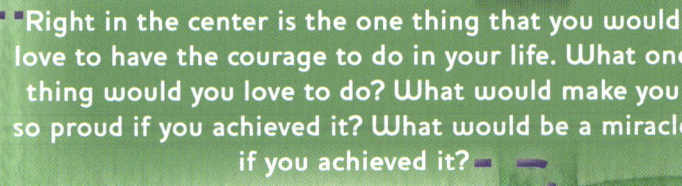

Right in the center is the one thing that you would love to have the courage to do in your life. What one thing would you love to do? What would make you so proud if you achieved it? What would be a miracle if you achieved it?

Walk through the Maze of Miracles and think about that one goal.

Walk into the

Maze of Miracles

START HERE

Imagine yourself doing it and succeeding with ease. Imagine others cheering you on. Imagine you are given a certificate or a trophy for your achievement.
Imagine others waving flags and shouting **'Congratulations'** and **'Well done'**.
Imagine how you would feel once you have achieved the one thing you were so scared of. How would you feel?

This is what my Maze of Miracles looks like

You can draw your Maze of Miracles here

You get closer and closer to the middle of the maze and closer and closer to achieving your own personal miracle. Finally you reach the center and you feel as if you have achieved what you set out to achieve. You can feel everyone congratulating you and imagine yourself holding the trophy or certificate. You feel amazing!

When you have walked through the amazing Maze of Miracles, you come out the other side and see that someone is waiting to speak to you.

It is now time for you to choose what you are going to do next. You can either take a step forward to meet your visitor or go back through the portal. If you choose to go back through the portal, take in a deep breath and breathe out slowly three times as you feel yourself coming back from your magical world, through the portal and back to the room.

To exit through the portal turn to page 186

Who would you like to meet?

To meet a WISE MAN, turn to page 105
To meet an ANGEL, turn to page 107
To meet a WIZARD, turn to page 109
To meet an ELF, turn to page 111
To meet a FORTUNE TELLER, turn to page 113
To meet a GENIE, turn to page 115
To meet the QUEEN OF HEARTS, turn to page 117
To meet your SPIRIT GUIDE turn to page 119
To meet a GODDESS, turn to page 121
To meet a SUPERHERO, turn to page 123

You find yourself in the **PALACE OF PEACE**

Everything in the Palace of Peace is calm and relaxing.
As soon as you step inside, you feel like being still and quiet.
Look around and on the walls you will see a variety of relaxing scenes from nature. One picture is a waterfall, another is of a calm lake.
There are also pictures of a beach and a wildflower field.
Take in a deep breath and breathe out slowly.

Palace of Peace

Relax your shoulders and feel the rest of your body relaxing.
Allow your eyes to soften as you look at a picture.
First of all notice the shapes. Let your eyes trace around the shape within the picture noticing all the tiny grooves and indentations in the paintwork.
Next, notice the colors in the picture. You might think at a glance that it is just one color, but colors are made up of other colors.
Can you spot any other colors? Notice the shades of color and how the light hits the picture. Notice the textures. Become fascinated with the picture. Sit as still as possible, only concentrating on the picture and let your mind become nice as still as you concentrate.

Notice how calm you feel after gazing at this peaceful picture.
As you look up, you see someone at the end of the long room.

This is what my PALACE OF PEACE looks like

You can draw your Palace of Peace here

It is now time for you to choose what you are going to do next.
You can either take a step forward to meet your visitor or go back
through the portal. If you choose to go back through the portal,
take in a deep breath and breathe out slowly three times as you
feel yourself coming back from your magical world, through the
portal and back to the room.

To exit through the portal turn to page 186

Who would you like to meet?

To meet a WISE MAN, turn to page 105
To meet an ANGEL, turn to page 107
To meet a WIZARD, turn to page 109
To meet an ELF, turn to page 111
To meet a FORTUNE TELLER, turn to page 113
To meet a GENIE, turn to page 115
To meet the QUEEN OF HEARTS, turn to page 117
To meet your SPIRIT GUIDE turn to page 119
To meet a GODDESS, turn to page 121
To meet a SUPERHERO, turn to page 123

START HERE

You see a

Wise Man

Standing infront of you.
The Wise Man is wearing a long robe
and has a beard and glasses.
He has a kind face and you feel very
safe in his company.
You instantly feel that he believes
in you and he wants the best
for you. He is here to
support and guide
you to be the best
you can possibly be.

The Wise Man is holding a book. In the book are a few words of
advice. The Wise Man is going to read out all the advice and he
wants you to pick one special sentence.

Be yourself, that is all you have to do.
It's OK to be YOU.
You are amazing and I believe in you.
Be kind and people will be kind to you.
You are unique.
Send all your worries to the moon.
Spend more time outside in nature.
Turn a cannot into a can.
You are good enough - just as you are.

You are amazing

Repeat this sentence in your mind
over and over again and think
about what it means to you.

The Wise Man has a gift for you. He points to ten boxes.
Each box has a gift tag with a symbol on it.
Choose a symbol and your gift.

Which Symbol will you choose?

Diamond - turn to page 125
Heart - turn to page 127
Leaf - turn to page 129
Circle - turn to page 131
Star - turn to page 133
Triangle - turn to page 135
Flower - turn to page 137
Spiral - turn to page 139
Sun - turn to page 141
Moon - turn to page 143

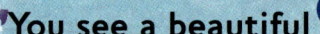

START HERE

You see a beautiful *Angel*

standing in front of you. It looks like it is made up of white light. The angel smiles at you and instantly make you feel safe and secure.

Your Angel wants you to know that you are protected at all times. You are safe and secure and so you don't need to worry. The Angel is looking out for you.

Stand opposite your Angel and look into its eyes.
Stand in the silence and let the angel send you feelings of love and care. You look into their eyes and you immediately feel precious and valuable. You feel that someone cares deeply for you.

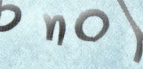

You are precious

Let the Angel stroke your face and back. Feel their warm hands of light all over your head and back. Their fingers of light feel so soft. You feel so safe and protected.

You feel safe and protected

After a while, the Angel stops
and brings you a beautiful box
with various drawers.
Each drawer has a symbol on it.
The Angel asks you to choose a
symbol and take what is inside
that drawer.

Which symbol will you choose?

Diamond - turn to page 125
Heart - turn to page 127
Leaf - turn to page 129
Circle - turn to page 131
Star - turn to page 133
Triangle - turn to page 135
Flower - turn to page 137
Spiral - turn to page 139
Sun - turn to page 141
Moon - turn to page 143

You see a

WIZARD

standing in front of you. The Wizard is wearing a long purple coat and matching hat. He has a big smile and is so pleased that you are meeting.

The Wizard has a magic trick for you. It is a trick to help change your mood when you are feeling anxious or scared or upset or lonely.

You are calm. You are safe

Think about how you are feeling. Stay very still and notice how you feel inside. Do you feel worried or scared or anxious or upset? Tell the Wizard on a scale of 1-10 how upset or sad you feel.

Activate the magic by rubbing your hands together very quickly. Next, copy the Wizard as you tap the center of your chest and you repeat an affirmation that will act as medicine for the feeling. For example, 'I am safe' could work for feeling scared, 'I am calm' could work for feeling anxious, and 'I am OK' could work for feeling sad. Keep tapping your chest as you repeat your special medicinal words.

NOW TAKE IN A DEEP BREATH AND

Do you notice any difference?
ON A SCALE OF 1-10,
how do you feel now?

The Wizard wants to give you a gift. He wants you to choose a gift by choosing a symbol. He hands you a box. Inside the box are ten envelopes with ten different symbols drawn on each envelope. Choose a symbol and you will receive your gift.

Which symbol will you choose?

Diamond - turn to page 125
Heart - turn to page 127
Leaf - turn to page 129
Circle - turn to page 131
Star - turn to page 133
Triangle - turn to page 135
Flower - turn to page 137
Spiral - turn to page 139
Sun - turn to page 141
Moon - turn to page 143

You see an

ELF

standing in front of you. The Elf has a happy face.
He loves smiling. The Elf wants to tell you the secret to
happiness. He tells you to shake all over to release lots of happy
feelings in your body.

Imagine yourself jumping up and
down and shaking.
Shake, shake, shake, and stop.
Notice how you feel.
Feel all the fizzy, happy energy
rushing all over your body.

Next, smile with the Elf. When you smile, your brain releases
positive chemicals all around your body that make you feel
happier and more joyful.

Join in the Elf's smiling game and see
how long you can smile for.
Turn the corners of your mouth up and
smile for as long as you can. Smile with
your eyes and even smile with your
tummy. When you have finished the
smiling game, notice how you feel.

The Elf wants to give you a gift. He wants you to choose a gift by choosing a symbol. He holds out a bag. Inside the bag are ten pebbles with ten different symbols drawn on each pebble.

Which Symbol will you choose?

Diamond - turn to page 125
Heart - turn to page 127
Leaf - turn to page 129
Circle - turn to page 131
Star - turn to page 133
Triangle - turn to page 135
Flower - turn to page 137
Spiral - turn to page 139
Sun - turn to page 141
Moon - turn to page 143

FORTUNE TELLER

...You see a

infront of you.
She is smiling, friendly
and approachable.

The Fortune Teller is shuffling a pack of cards, and one of the cards is for you. She will read them out and you just have to say **Stop** when you want to choose a card.

You will be very lucky this year.
You are moving towards great things, new horizons
and fantastic opportunities.
Good fortune will come to you soon.
You will have a very happy and comfortable year.
You will make new friends this year
Great things are coming to you.

You think about what the Fortune Teller has said and
feel full of excitement about the future.
You feel positive about your future.
You know good things will happen.

The Fortune Teller shows you her crystal ball. Look inside the crystal ball and you
see it is clouded over. Slowly the cloud disappears and a symbol appears before
your eyes. Let the Fortune Teller know what you see.

What Symbol can you see?

Diamond - turn to page 125
Heart - turn to page 127
Leaf - turn to page 129
Circle - turn to page 131
Star - turn to page 133
Triangle - turn to page 135
Flower - turn to page 137
Spiral - turn to page 139
Sun - turn to page 141
Moon - turn to page 143

START HERE

GENIE

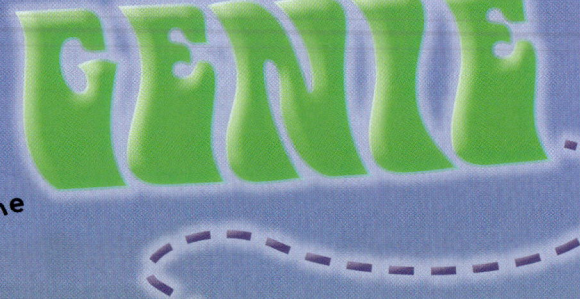

You stand in front of the

He is smiling.
The Genie only wants good things for you.

The Genie asks you to stand very still and think about how you feel inside? How does your body feel? Can you feel any feelings in your body? How does your mind feel? Do you feel relaxed or tense?
The Genie now asks you to make a wish. What do you wish for? Would you like to feel more peaceful inside? Would you like to feel more joy in your head? Would you like to feel more relaxed in your stomach? Would you like to feel more love in your heart? What do you wish for? Make your wish and watch the Genie sprinkle you with golden dust.
Stay quiet and notice how you feel. Do you feel any change?

The Genie has a gift for you. He throws ten colored scarves in the air and asks you to catch one. Each scarf has a different symbol on it. Which scarf did you catch?

You are magical

WHICH SYMBOL IS ON YOUR SCARF?

Diamond - turn to page 125
Heart - turn to page 127
Leaf - turn to page 129
Circle - turn to page 131
Star - turn to page 133
Triangle - turn to page 135
Flower - turn to page 137
Spiral - turn to page 139
Sun - turn to page 141
Moon - turn to page 143

START HERE

Meet the Queen of hearts

She is dressed in red hearts from top to toe. You can see from her face that she has such a kind heart. She is interested in your heart and how you feel and wants to help you feel better.

The Queen of Hearts asks you to put your hands in the middle of your chest and imagine there is a pink light there. The pink light gets brighter and brighter and is expanding and getting bigger and bigger. The bigger the heart gets, the more you feel full of love and good feeling for yourself and others. You have good thoughts for yourself, your family, your friends, your neighbors and all those who live close by.

Diamond - turn to page 125
Heart - turn to page 127
Leaf - turn to page 129
Circle - turn to page 131
Star - turn to page 133
Triangle - turn to page 135
Flower - turn to page 137
Spiral - turn to page 139
Sun - turn to page 141
Moon - turn to page 143

The Queen of Hearts has a gift for you. She shows you a tray of jam tarts. Each tart has a symbol on top.

Choose a symbol and your gift.

As the pink light gets bigger, you start to have good feelings for people you don't know so well. You have good feelings for animals and birds and all people and creatures on the Earth. It feels so good to have a heart full of good feeling.

START HERE

Your *Spirit Guide* **is standing infront of you.**

What does your Spirit Guide look like?

Is your Spirit Guide a she or he?

Your Spirit Guide is here to show you how to find **inner pe**ace, inner calm and in**ner hap**piness. You notice they **are hold**ing something in their hand. They give you a box. It is a box of bottles. Inside eac**h bottle is a positive feeling th**at they have captured fr**om nat**ure. There is happiness from sunshine, calm from moonlight, freedom from fresh air. Take each bottle in turn, take off the lid and let all the feelings come out and surround you.

Take the sunshine bottle and unscrew the lid. Feel all the yellow sunshine feelings spill out of the bottle, into the room and into your whole body. Breathe in the sunshine, then screw the lid tight and place it back.

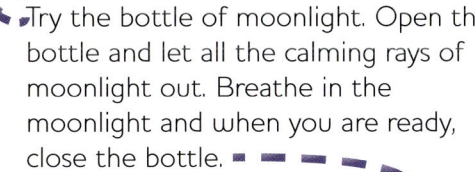

Try the bottle of moonlight. Open the bottle and let all the calming rays of moonlight out. Breathe in the moonlight and when you are ready, close the bottle.

Open the bottle of fresh air and let that fresh air move around the room and all over your body. Feel your lungs filling up with fresh air as you breathe it in. You feel so fresh and free. When you are ready, close the bottle. Your Spirit Guide is giving you these bottles as a gift. They have bottled up these special feelings for you to use any time you need them. Keep them safe.

Your Spirit Guide has another special gift for you. They ask you to choose a symbol to reveal your gift. Which symbol do you choose?

Diamond - turn to page 125
Heart - turn to page 127
Leaf - turn to page 129
Circle - turn to page 131
Star - turn to page 133
Triangle - turn to page 135
Flower - turn to page 137
Spiral - turn to page 139
Sun - turn to page 141
Moon - turn to page 143

You are calm. You are happy. You are calm. You are peaceful

START HERE

Standing in front of you is a GODDESS

She is wearing a long satin and velvet dress and is very beautiful.
She would like to be your mentor and take care of you.
The Goddess is surrounded by herbs and potions.
She knows how to make medicine out of leaves and flowers she finds in nature. She has made up some emotion potions for you.
Whenever you feel sad or gloomy, anxious or upset, you can take an emotion potion and the herbs will gently work, making you feel better.
She has a bottle of lemon balm to help you feel calm, a bottle of chamomile to help you when you feel upset and a bottle of passion flower for when you feel sad. Which potion would you like to keep with you? Whenever you feel you need the potion, you just have to take one drop and put it in a cup of warm drink and it should help you feel better.

**Take the potion and take a deep breath
in as you breathe in the lovely aroma and
breathe out slowly.**

The Goddess has a magical gift for you.
She shows you her table.
On the table are ten wooden
symbols. She asks you to choose one.
Which symbol do you choose?

You are calm, you are happy

Which gift would you like?

Diamond – turn to page 125
Heart – turn to page 127
Leaf – turn to page 129
Circle – turn to page 131
Star – turn to page 133
Triangle – turn to page 135
Flower – turn to page 137
Spiral – turn to page 139
Sun – turn to page 141
Moon – turn to page 143

START HERE

Standing in front of you is a

SUPERHERO

The Superhero is very friendly and always has time for you. He would like to be your mentor and take care of you. The Superhero knows that you are a young superhero in training and he is going to show you all his superpowers.

In situations where people are annoying you, you just have to use your superhero deep breath power and breathe in and out slowly. When others make nasty comments, your superhero will remind you to be strong and remember your inner power and confidence and let the words wash off you. Your superhero wants to show you a great trick to help you feel confident. Make a power pose. Stand up tall with your hands on your hips and feel powerful and confident in your body. Notice how this affects your mind and you start to feel confident inside.

You start to feel confident

The Superhero has a gift for you. He turns around and you see ten different symbols on his cloak. Choose a symbol to find out which gift is for you.

Choose a symbol to find out which gift is for you.

Remember your inner power

Diamond - turn to page 125
Heart - turn to page 127
Leaf - turn to page 129
Circle - turn to page 131
Star - turn to page 133
Triangle - turn to page 135
Flower - turn to page 137
Spiral - turn to page 139
Sun - turn to page 141
Moon - turn to page 143

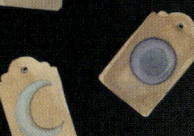

Your gift is a **BOX OF LOVE.**

How big is the box? The box is full of love.
How does it feel to be holding love in your hands? Can you see the love? What color is it? How does it feel? How does it sound? Can you see inside the box? What is inside the Box of Love? How does this love make you feel? What does love mean to you? Would you like to have more love in your life? How can you create more love for yourself?
How can you increase your feelings of love? Do you feel full of love? Take a deep breath in and breathe out slowly. Breathe in, breathe out. Breathe in and say, "I am loving". Breathe out and say, "I am loving".

Your visitor wants to give you a positive Mood Card.

This will help you stay in a positive mood for the rest of the day.
Would you like to carry on and get your positive mood card, or would you like to go back through the portal and go back to the room? If you would like to go back, take in a deep breath and go through the portal.
To exit through the portal turn to page 186.
If you would like to go on, **Pick a number to reveal your mood card.**

Pick a Number:

NUMBER 01 - turn to page 146
NUMBER 02 - turn to page 148
NUMBER 03 - turn to page 150
NUMBER 04 - turn to page 152
NUMBER 05 - turn to page 154
NUMBER 06 - turn to page 156
NUMBER 07 - turn to page 158
NUMBER 08 - turn to page 160
NUMBER 09 - turn to page 162
NUMBER 10 - turn to page 164

Your gift is a

Hold the Heart of Gratitude in your hands. Can you feel your Heart of Gratitude? Gratitude is being grateful. Gratitude is being thankful. The Heart of Gratitude notices everything wonderful about your life. Your Heart of Gratitude sees what is special.
The Heart of Gratitude appreciates all the little things in life.
The more your Heart of Gratitude is thankful, the bigger it grows.
Feel your Heart of Gratitude growing bigger and bigger.
Your Heart of Gratitude becomes so big that there is no longer any room for upset or complaint.

Each moment, you notice all the wonderful things in your life. Everything makes you smile. What are you grateful for? What do you give thanks for?
Make a long list of everything you love. Note everything that you appreciate. The more you use your Heart of Gratitude, the bigger your heart will grow and the happier you will be. Take a deep breath in and breathe out slowly. Breathe in, breathe out.

Your visitor wants to give you a positive Mood Card.

This will help you stay in a positive mood for the rest of the day.
Would you like to carry on and get your positive mood card, or would you like to go back through the portal and go back to the room? If you would like to go back, take in a deep breath and go through the portal.
To exit through the portal turn to page 186.
If you would like to go on, **Pick a number to reveal your mood card.**

Pick a Number:

NUMBER 01 - turn to page 146
NUMBER 02 - turn to page 148
NUMBER 03 - turn to page 150
NUMBER 04 - turn to page 152
NUMBER 05 - turn to page 154
NUMBER 06 - turn to page 156
NUMBER 07 - turn to page 158
NUMBER 08 - turn to page 160
NUMBER 09 - turn to page 162
NUMBER 10 - turn to page 164

Your gift is a **BOTTLE OF COURAGE.**

Courage is feeling strong and powerful. Courage is believing in yourself and trying your best. Courage is doing your best. Courage is being the best you can be. Holding onto this bottle helps you remember to have courage and be brave. Take in a deep breath. Breathe in a feeling of strength and courage. Feel the courage in your legs.

They take you to new places and give you the confidence to walk tall. Feel the courage in your arms. They give you the courage to try new things. Feel courage in your head. It gives you the confidence to believe in yourself. Continue to hold onto your Bottle of Courage and feel courage growing all over your body. Drink from your Bottle of Courage every day. Feel yourself getting taller and taller, stronger and stronger, and full of courage. Say to yourself, I am full of courage. I am full of courage. I am full of courage.

Your visitor wants to give you a positive Mood Card

This will help you stay in a positive mood for the rest of the day. Would you like to carry on and get your positive mood card, or would you like to go back through the portal and go back to the room? If you would like to go back, take in a deep breath and go through the portal.
To exit through the portal turn to page 186
If you would like to go on,
Pick a number to reveal your mood card.

Pick a Number:

NUMBER 01 - turn to page 146
NUMBER 02 - turn to page 148
NUMBER 03 - turn to page 150
NUMBER 04 - turn to page 152
NUMBER 05 - turn to page 154
NUMBER 06 - turn to page 156
NUMBER 07 - turn to page 158
NUMBER 08 - turn to page 160
NUMBER 09 - turn to page 162
NUMBER 10 - turn to page 164

A little Bottle of Courage

Your gift is a pair of

SHOES OF CONFIDENCE.

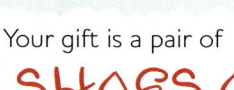

Put the shoes on. How do they feel on your feet? Are they heavy or light on your feet? Feel your toes in your Shoes of Confidence.

How do they feel? Can you feel each individual toe? How does it feel? Can you feel the bottom of the shoes? Wiggle your feet and stretch your toes in your Shoes of Confidence.

Your Shoes of Confidence help your feet feel so confident.

This confidence is spreading up through your legs. You feel your legs moving with confidence. The confident feeling is now moving up through your spine. Your spine is growing tall as you feel full of confidence. You feel the confidence moving through your arms and head and mind. Your mind is confident. You believe in yourself and feel confident. Imagine you are walking around wearing your Shoes of Confidence. Feel yourself taking long, confident strides. You feel OK. You feel strong. You feel good about yourself. The shoes make you feel great. You can put these shoes on when you need a boost of confidence.

Repeat to yourself in your mind, I am confident. I am good. I am special. I am OK. I believe in myself. I can do it. I am calm and in control.

Your visitor wants to give you a positive Mood Card

Your visitor wants to give you a positive Mood Card. This will help you stay in a positive mood for the rest of the day. Would you like to carry on and get your positive mood card, or would you like to go back through the portal and go back to the room? If you would like to go back, take in a deep breath and go through the portal. **To exit through the portal turn to page 186**

If you would like to go on,

Pick a number to reveal your mood card.

Pick a Number:

NUMBER 01 - turn to page 146
NUMBER 02 - turn to page 148
NUMBER 03 - turn to page 150
NUMBER 04 - turn to page 152
NUMBER 05 - turn to page 154
NUMBER 06 - turn to page 156
NUMBER 07 - turn to page 158
NUMBER 08 - turn to page 160
NUMBER 09 - turn to page 162
NUMBER 10 - turn to page 164

Your gift is the BOOK OF WISDOM.

Hold the book in your hands.
How big is your book?
How many pages does it have?
What color is the book?
Are there any pictures in the book?

This is your Book of Wisdom.
The Book of Wisdom answers all your questions. It is full of all the answers you will ever need.
Do you have a question?
What would you like to know?
Stay very still and look at your Book of Wisdom.
Open the book at random and see what the answer to your question is. It might be a word or a picture or even a feeling.

What picture do you see on the page? What words do you see on the page? What does this mean to you? How does it make you feel?
The Book of Wisdom is a great gift as it reminds you that all the answers to all your questions come from inside you. You have all the answers.

Repeat to yourself, "I am wise, I am wise."

Your visitor wants to give you a positive Mood Card.

You are wise, You are wise

START HERE

This will help you stay in a positive mood for the rest of the day. Would you like to carry on and get your positive mood card, or would you like to go back through the portal and go back to the room? If you would like to go back, take in a deep breath and go through the portal.

To exit through the portal turn to page 186
If you would like to go on,
Pick a number to reveal your mood card.

Pick a Number:

NUMBER 01 - turn to page 146
NUMBER 02 - turn to page 148
NUMBER 03 - turn to page 150
NUMBER 04 - turn to page 152
NUMBER 05 - turn to page 154
NUMBER 06 - turn to page 156
NUMBER 07 - turn to page 158
NUMBER 08 - turn to page 160
NUMBER 09 - turn to page 162
NUMBER 10 - turn to page 164

Your gift is a

CUP OF JOY.

Look into your Cup of Joy.
How full is it? Is it full?
Is it half-full or half-empty?
If you would like to fill your
cup, you can pour more joy
into your cup. Take in a deep
breath of joy and happiness
and breathe out joy into your
cup. Notice how the cup fills
up with a wonderful feeling
of happiness and joy.

Say to yourself, I am joyful and happy.
I am joyful and happy. My cup is full of joy, my mind is full of joy,
my heart is full of joy and my body is full of joy . Imagine yourself doing
the things that make you feel joyful. Hold your Cup of Joy and feel full to
the brim with joy and happiness.

Your visitor wants to give you a positive Mood Card.

This will help you stay in a positive mood for the rest of the day.
Would you like to carry on and get your positive mood card, or would you like to
go back through the portal and go back to the room?
If you would like to go back, take in a deep breath and go through the portal.
To exit through the portal turn to page 186
If you would like to go on,
Pick a number to reveal your mood card.

You are joyful, you are joyful

Pick a Number:

NUMBER 01 - turn to page 146
NUMBER 02 - turn to page 148
NUMBER 03 - turn to page 150
NUMBER 04 - turn to page 152
NUMBER 05 - turn to page 154
NUMBER 06 - turn to page 156
NUMBER 07 - turn to page 158
NUMBER 08 - turn to page 160
NUMBER 09 - turn to page 162
NUMBER 10 - turn to page 164

START HERE

Your gift is a

KEY OF LUCK.

You are very lucky to have a Key of Luck. Take it with you wherever you go and it will bring you luck with every step. Do you know what luck is? Luck is good fortune. Luck is when wonderful things happen that you didn't expect. If you carry your Key of Luck, you will find luck behind every door. You will find luck around every corner. Luck will follow you. Do you feel lucky? If you believe, you will become very lucky.

If you carry your Key of Luck, lucky things will happen to you. You are lucky. Good things always happen to you.

You are fortunate and special things happen to you. Your life is blessed. You are blessed with good luck. You attract good luck to you. You will always be lucky and fortunate. Amazing and wonderful things always happen for you. What lucky things would you like to happen? Stay very still and imagine those lucky things happening to you.

Repeat to yourself over and over again, I am lucky. I am lucky. I am lucky. I am lucky. I am lucky. I am lucky.

Your visitor wants to give you a positive Mood Card.

You are lucky, you are lucky, you are lucky

This will help you stay in a positive mood for the rest of the day.

Would you like to carry on and get your positive mood card, or would you like to go back through the portal and go back to the room?

If you would like to go back, take in a deep breath and go through the portal.

To exit through the portal turn to page 186

If you would like to go on,

Pick a number to reveal your mood card.

Pick a Number:

NUMBER 01 - turn to page 146
NUMBER 02 - turn to page 148
NUMBER 03 - turn to page 150
NUMBER 04 - turn to page 152
NUMBER 05 - turn to page 154
NUMBER 06 - turn to page 156
NUMBER 07 - turn to page 158
NUMBER 08 - turn to page 160
NUMBER 09 - turn to page 162
NUMBER 10 - turn to page 164

Your gift is a BAG OF KINDNESS.

Hold the bag in your hands.
How does the bag feel?
The Bag of Kindness has lots of ideas inside that you can use to show kindness to those around you. Stay very still and listen to all the ideas and see which one you are going to try today.

Here are all the kindness ideas from inside the Bag of Kindness:

Say good morning.
Give someone a compliment.
Help cook dinner. Say please.
Color a picture and give it to someone. Write a letter.
Say thank you.
Make a new friend. Tidy your room. Smile.
Be positive to bus drivers, shop assistants and people who work in the community. Invite a friend for tea. Bake a cake.
Hold the door open for someone. Help a friend with their work.
Visit an elderly neighbor. What are you going to do today?

Stay still and choose one thing from inside the Bag of Kindness.
Imagine you are doing that kind action and notice how it makes you feel about yourself. Feel yourself smiling inside.

Your visitor wants to give you a positive Mood Card.

This will help you stay in a positive mood for the rest of the day.

Would you like to carry on and get your positive mood card, or would you like to go back through the portal and go back to the room?
If you would like to go back, take in a deep breath and go through the portal.
To exit through the portal turn to page 186
If you would like to go on,
Pick a number to reveal your mood card.

Bag of
Kindness

Pick a Number:

NUMBER 01 - turn to page 146
NUMBER 02 - turn to page 148
NUMBER 03 - turn to page 150
NUMBER 04 - turn to page 152
NUMBER 05 - turn to page 154
NUMBER 06 - turn to page 156
NUMBER 07 - turn to page 158
NUMBER 08 - turn to page 160
NUMBER 09 - turn to page 162
NUMBER 10 - turn to page 164

Your gift is a

LIGHT POD.

This is a special pod that you can sit inside when you feel a little moody, sad or down. The multi-colored lights in this pod can help lift your mood. When your skin and eyes absorb the colored light, it can help you feel better in your mind and body. Step into the pod and switch the light on. Stay very still and allow the light to soak into your body. First of all, notice the red light all around you.

This red light helps you feel strong, grounded and full of energy. Allow the red light to sink into your skin and help you feel strong. The light is now switching to orange. This orange light helps you feel happy, bright and full of creativity. Feel the rays from the orange light sinking through your skin and lighting up all your cells inside, helping you feel brighter. The light is now switching to yellow.
This helps you feel more balanced and healthy.
Feel the bright yellow light moving into your body.

It feels wonderful. The light is now switching to green and then blue. These two colors help relax your nerves and help you feel calm.
Feel the soft light calming you down. The light is now switching to indigo and then violet. This helps you relax deeply and helps you have beautiful dreams. Allow yourself to relax and let go as you enjoy the healing colors sink into your skin.

Your visitor wants to give you a positive Mood Card.

This will help you stay in a positive mood for the rest of the day.
Would you like to carry on and get your positive mood card, or would you like
to go back through the portal and go back to the room?
If you would like to go back, take in a deep breath and go through the portal.

**To exit through the
portal turn to page 186**
If you would like to go on,
Pick a number to reveal your mood card.

Pick a Number:

NUMBER 01 - turn to page 146
NUMBER 02 - turn to page 148
NUMBER 03 - turn to page 150
NUMBER 04 - turn to page 152
NUMBER 05 - turn to page 154
NUMBER 06 - turn to page 156
NUMBER 07 - turn to page 158
NUMBER 08 - turn to page 160
NUMBER 09 - turn to page 162
NUMBER 10 - turn to page 164

Your gift is a

CLOAK OF PROTECTION.

Put the cloak around your shoulders. How does the cloak feel against your shoulders, back and arms? Stay very still and feel the softness of the cloak.

This is your Cloak of Protection. This cloak protects you from hurtful words and comments from others. The cloak protects you from unpleasant, upsetting and uncomfortable situations.

The Cloak of Protection protects you from harm. Whenever you need your Cloak of Protection, you just have to wrap it around your body and mind, and you will feel totally safe and warm inside. Stay still and feel safe wrapped up in your Cloak of Protection. Repeat to yourself,

I am OK. I am safe. I am protected. I am secure.
I am free from danger. I am secure.

If anyone tries to hurt you with unkind words or actions, the words just bounce off the cloak and you feel strong, unhurt and unharmed by their nastiness. Nothing can touch you. How do you feel now?

Do you feel a tingly feeling of strength and protection in your body? Do you feel OK? Do you feel safe? Take in a deep breath and breathe in strength, and breathe out power. Breathe in strength and breathe out power. Remember, you can put on your Cloak of Protection whenever you need it.

Your visitor wants to give you a positive Mood Card.

This will help you stay in a positive mood for the rest of the day.

Pick a Number:

NUMBER 01 - turn to page 146
NUMBER 02 - turn to page 148
NUMBER 03 - turn to page 150
NUMBER 04 - turn to page 152
NUMBER 05 - turn to page 154
NUMBER 06 - turn to page 156
NUMBER 07 - turn to page 158
NUMBER 08 - turn to page 160
NUMBER 09 - turn to page 162
NUMBER 10 - turn to page 164

Would you like to carry on and get your positive mood card, or would you like to go back through the portal and go back to the room?
If you would like to go back, take in a deep breath and go through the portal.

To exit through the portal turn to page 186

If you would like to go on,

Pick a number to reveal your mood card.

To choose the Plum Key go to page 166
To choose the Orange Key go to page 168
To choose the Purple Key go to page 170
To choose the Pink Key go to Page 172
To choose the Black Key go to page 174
To choose the White Key go to page 176
To choose the Green Key go to page 178
To choose the Aqua Key go to page 180
To choose the Yellow Key go to page 182
To choose the Blue Key go to page 184

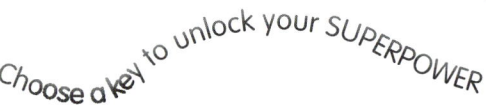

Choose a key to unlock your SUPERPOWER

It is time to collect your **SUPERPOWER.**
This **SUPERPOWER** will remind you to be
strong and in control of your life.
Once you have collected your **SUPERPOWER,**
you can take it with your gift, **MOOD CARD** and
all the special lessons you have learnt on your
magical adventure.

Once you have your positive Mood Card,
repeat the words as many times as you can.
It is now time to collect your final item
before you go back through the portal.

Here is your positive **MOOD CARD**

"Today I will be
Happy like a Bumble Bee ♥"

Spend some time looking at it, thinking about what it means,
and how you can get into that positive mood.

To choose the Plum Key go to page 166
To choose the Orange Key go to page 168
To choose the Purple Key go to page 170
To choose the Pink Key go to Page 172
To choose the Black Key go to page 174
To choose the White Key go to page 176
To choose the Green Key go to page 178
To choose the Aqua Key go to page 180
To choose the Yellow Key go to page 182
To choose the Blue Key go to page 184

Choose a key to unlock your SUPERPOWER

It is time to collect your **SUPERPOWER**.
This **SUPERPOWER** will remind you to be
strong and in control of your life.
Once you have collected your **SUPERPOWER**,
you can take it with your gift, **MOOD CARD**
and all the special lessons you have learnt on your
magical adventure.

Once you have your positive Mood Card,
repeat the words as many times as you can.
It is now time to collect your final item
before you go back through the portal.

START HERE

02 You picked NUMBER TWO.

Here is your positive **MOOD CARD**

Today I will be... determined like a rocket

Spend some time looking at it, thinking about what it means, and how you can get into that positive mood.

To choose the Plum Key go to page 166
To choose the Orange Key go to page 168
To choose the Purple Key go to page 170
To choose the Pink Key go to Page 172
To choose the Black Key go to page 174
To choose the White Key go to page 176
To choose the Green Key go to page 178
To choose the Aqua Key go to page 180
To choose the Yellow Key go to page 182
To choose the Blue Key go to page 184

Choose a key to unlock your SUPERPOWER

It is time to collect your **SUPERPOWER**.
This **SUPERPOWER** will remind you to be
strong and in control of your life.
Once you have collected your **SUPERPOWER,**
you can take it with your gift, **MOOD CARD**
and all the special lessons you have learnt on
your magical adventure.

Once you have your positive Mood Card,
repeat the words as many times as you can.
It is now time to collect your final item
before you go back through the portal.

Here is your positive MOOD CARD

Today I will be...

Confident like a GIANT

Spend some time looking at it, thinking about what it means, and how you can get into that positive mood.

To choose the Plum Key go to page 166
To choose the Orange Key go to page 168
To choose the Purple Key go to page 170
To choose the Pink Key go to Page 172
To choose the Black Key go to page 174
To choose the White Key go to page 176
To choose the Green Key go to page 178
To choose the Aqua Key go to page 180
To choose the Yellow Key go to page 182
To choose the Blue Key go to page 184

Choose a key to unlock your SUPERPOWER

It is time to collect your **SUPERPOWER**. This **SUPERPOWER** will remind you to be strong and in control of your life.
Once you have collected your **SUPERPOWER**, you can take it with your gift, **MOOD CARD** and all the special lessons you have learnt on your magical adventure.

Once you have your positive Mood Card, repeat the words as many times as you can. It is now time to collect your final item before you go back through the portal.

04 You picked NUMBER FOUR

Here is your positive **MOOD CARD**

START HERE

Today I will be . . .

Cheerful . . .

like a bubbling stream

Spend some time looking at it, thinking about what it means, and how you can get into that positive mood.

To choose the Plum Key go to page 166
To choose the Orange Key go to page 168
To choose the Purple Key go to page 170
To choose the Pink Key go to Page 172
To choose the Black Key go to page 174
To choose the White Key go to page 176
To choose the Green Key go to page 178
To choose the Aqua Key go to page 180
To choose the Yellow Key go to page 182
To choose the Blue Key go to page 184

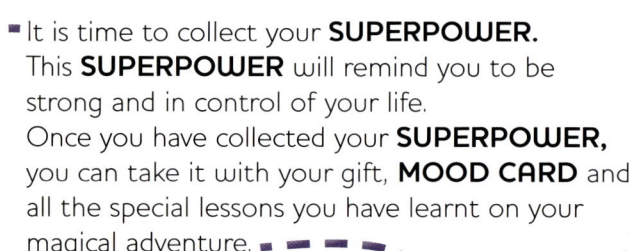

It is time to collect your **SUPERPOWER.**
This **SUPERPOWER** will remind you to be strong and in control of your life.
Once you have collected your **SUPERPOWER,** you can take it with your gift, **MOOD CARD** and all the special lessons you have learnt on your magical adventure.

Once you have your positive Mood Card, repeat the words as many times as you can. It is now time to collect your final item before you go back through the portal.

You picked NUMBER FIVE

Here is your positive **MOOD CARD**

Today I will be... Courageous... like a lion ♥♥♥

Spend some time looking at it, thinking about what it means, and how you can get into that positive mood.

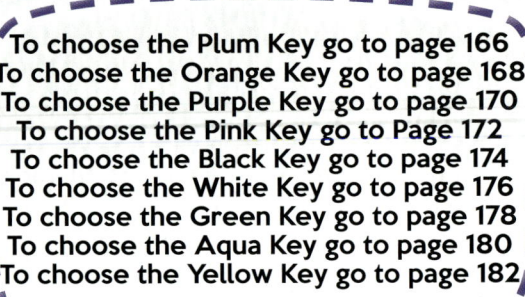

To choose the Plum Key go to page 166
To choose the Orange Key go to page 168
To choose the Purple Key go to page 170
To choose the Pink Key go to Page 172
To choose the Black Key go to page 174
To choose the White Key go to page 176
To choose the Green Key go to page 178
To choose the Aqua Key go to page 180
To choose the Yellow Key go to page 182
To choose the Blue Key go to page 184

It is time to collect your **SUPERPOWER.**
This **SUPERPOWER** will remind you to
bestrong and in control of your life.
Once you have collected your **SUPERPOWER,**
you can take it with your gift, **MOOD CARD**
and all the special lessons you have learnt on
your magical adventure.

Once you have your positive Mood Card,
repeat the words as many times as you can.
It is now time to collect your final item
before you go back through the portal.

Here is your positive **MOOD CARD**

Spend some time looking at it, thinking about what it means, and how you can get into that positive mood.

To choose the Plum Key go to page 166
To choose the Orange Key go to page 168
To choose the Purple Key go to page 170
To choose the Pink Key go to Page 172
To choose the Black Key go to page 174
To choose the White Key go to page 176
To choose the Green Key go to page 178
To choose the Aqua Key go to page 180
To choose the Yellow Key go to page 182
To choose the Blue Key go to page 184

It is time to collect your **SUPERPOWER.**
This **SUPERPOWER** will remind you to be strong and
in control of your life.
Once you have collected your **SUPERPOWER,**
you can take it with your gift, **MOOD CARD** and all
the special lessons you have learnt on your magical
adventure.

Once you have your positive Mood Card,
repeat the words as many times as you can.
It is now time to collect your final item
before you go back through the portal.

Here is your positive **MOOD CARD**

Today I will be...

Peaceful

... like a lake

Spend some time looking at it, thinking about what it means, and how you can get into that positive mood.

To choose the Plum Key go to page 166
To choose the Orange Key go to page 168
To choose the Purple Key go to page 170
To choose the Pink Key go to Page 172
To choose the Black Key go to page 174
To choose the White Key go to page 176
To choose the Green Key go to page 178
To choose the Aqua Key go to page 180
To choose the Yellow Key go to page 182
To choose the Blue Key go to page 184

It is time to collect your **SUPERPOWER.**
This **SUPERPOWER** will remind you to be strong
and in control of your life.
Once you have collected your **SUPERPOWER,**
you can take it with your gift, **MOOD CARD** and all
the special lessons you have learnt on your magical
adventure.

Once you have your positive Mood Card,
repeat the words as many times as you can.
It is now time to collect your final item
before you go back through the portal.

START HERE

08 You picked NUMBER EIGHT

Here is your positive **MOOD CARD**

Today I will be

Calm

like the breeze...

Spend some time looking at it, thinking about what it means,
and how you can get into that positive mood.

To choose the Plum Key go to page 166
To choose the Orange Key go to page 168
To choose the Purple Key go to page 170
To choose the Pink Key go to Page 172
To choose the Black Key go to page 174
To choose the White Key go to page 176
To choose the Green Key go to page 178
To choose the Aqua Key go to page 180
To choose the Yellow Key go to page 182
To choose the Blue Key go to page 184

It is time to collect your **SUPERPOWER**.
This **SUPERPOWER** will remind you to be strong and in control of your life.
Once you have collected your **SUPERPOWER**, you can take it with your gift, **MOOD CARD** and all the special lessons you have learnt on your magical adventure.

Once you have your positive Mood Card, repeat the words as many times as you can. It is now time to collect your final item before you go back through the portal.

Here is your positive **MOOD CARD**

Today I will be playful like a monkey

Spend some time looking at it, thinking about what it means, and how you can get into that positive mood.

To choose the Plum Key go to page 166
To choose the Orange Key go to page 168
To choose the Purple Key go to page 170
To choose the Pink Key go to Page 172
To choose the Black Key go to page 174
To choose the White Key go to page 176
To choose the Green Key go to page 178
To choose the Aqua Key go to page 180
To choose the Yellow Key go to page 182
To choose the Blue Key go to page 184

It is time to collect your **SUPERPOWER.**
This **SUPERPOWER** will remind you to be strong and
in control of your life.
Once you have collected your **SUPERPOWER,**
you can take it with your gift, **MOOD CARD** and all
the special lessons you have learnt on your magical
adventure.

Once you have your positive Mood Card,
repeat the words as many times as you can.
It is now time to collect your final item
before you go back through the portal.

Here is your positive **MOOD CARD**

Today I will be...

Strong like stone.

Spend some time looking at it, thinking about what it means,
and how you can get into that positive mood.

Your **SUPERPOWER** IS......

STRENGTH

Look at your SUPERPOWER and feel it inside.
Breathe in and feel the SUPERPOWER starting to work.

Now with your **SUPERPOWER** you can choose to go back through the portal or if you would like to collect more gifts, messages and superpowers, you can continue your adventure in new and exciting lands. If you would like to go back to the portal, take in a deep breath and blow out slowly. Feel yourself disappearing from this magical land and re-appearing back in your room. You may need to try three deep breaths to get you back to the room.

You find a magic key that leads to a room.
In the room is a huge cinema screen.
The curtains are closed.
You notice the curtains slowly opening to
reveal your **SUPERPOWER.**

You are strong

If you would like to choose a new mode of transport to take you
to the next part of your magical journey, make your choice now.

To fly on a MAGIC CARPET, turn to page 25
To travel in a PRIVATE JET, turn to page 27
To fly on your own UNICORN, turn to page 29
To travel in a HOT AIR BALLOON, turn to page 31
To travel in a TIME MACHINE, turn to page 33
To use magic INVISIBILITY DUST, turn to page 35
To travel by BOAT, turn to page 37
To fly on a HOVER BOARD, turn to page 39
To fly on a BROOMSTICK, turn to page 41
To travel in a ROCKET, turn to page 43

If you have completed your magical journey,
Please go to page 186

Your **SUPERPOWER** IS......

RESILIENCE

Look at your SUPERPOWER and feel it inside.
Breathe in and feel the SUPERPOWER starting to work.

Now with your **SUPERPOWER** you can choose to go back through the portal or if you would like to collect more gifts, messages and superpowers, you can continue your adventure in new and exciting lands. If you would like to go back to the portal, take in a deep breath and blow out slowly. Feel yourself disappearing from this magical land and re-appearing back in your room. You may need to try three deep breaths to get you back to the room.

You are resilient

You find a magic key that leads to a room.
In the room is a huge cinema screen.
The curtains are closed.
You notice the curtains slowly opening to
reveal your **SUPERPOWER.**

If you would like to choose a new mode of transport to take you
to the next part of your magical journey, make your choice now.

To fly on a MAGIC CARPET, turn to page 25
To travel in a PRIVATE JET, turn to page 27
To fly on your own UNICORN, turn to page 29
To travel in a HOT AIR BALLOON, turn to page 31
To travel in a TIME MACHINE, turn to page 33
To use magic INVISIBILITY DUST, turn to page 35
To travel by BOAT, turn to page 37
To fly on a HOVER BOARD, turn to page 39
To fly on a BROOMSTICK, turn to page 41
To travel in a ROCKET, turn to page 43

**If you have completed your magical journey,
Please go to page 186**

Your **SUPERPOWER** IS......

CONFIDENCE

Look at your SUPERPOWER and feel it inside.
Breathe in and feel the SUPERPOWER starting to work.

Now with your **SUPERPOWER** you can choose to go back through the portal or if you would like to collect more gifts, messages and superpowers, you can continue your adventure in new and exciting lands. If you would like to go back to the portal, take in a deep breath and blow out slowly. Feel yourself disappearing from this magical land and re-appearing back in your room. You may need to try three deep breaths to get you back to the room.

You find a magic key that leads to a room.
In the room is a huge cinema screen.
The curtains are closed.
You notice the curtains slowly opening to
reveal your **SUPERPOWER.**

START

You are confident

If you would like to choose a new mode of transport to take you
to the next part of your magical journey, make your choice now.

To fly on a MAGIC CARPET, turn to page 25
To travel in a PRIVATE JET, turn to page 27
To fly on your own UNICORN, turn to page 29
To travel in a HOT AIR BALLOON, turn to page 31
To travel in a TIME MACHINE, turn to page 33
To use magic INVISIBILITY DUST, turn to page 35
To travel by BOAT, turn to page 37
To fly on a HOVER BOARD, turn to page 39
To fly on a BROOMSTICK, turn to page 41
To travel in a ROCKET, turn to page 43

If you have completed your magical journey,
Please go to page 186

Your **SUPERPOWER** IS.......

KINDNESS

Look at your SUPERPOWER and feel it inside.
Breathe in and feel the SUPERPOWER starting to work.

Now with your **SUPERPOWER** you can choose to go back through the portal or if you would like to collect more gifts, messages and superpowers, you can continue your adventure in new and exciting lands. If you would like to go back to the portal, take in a deep breath and blow out slowly. Feel yourself disappearing from this magical land and re-appearing back in your room. You may need to try three deep breaths to get you back to the room.

You find a magic key that leads to a room.
In the room is a huge cinema screen.
The curtains are closed.
You notice the curtains slowly opening to
reveal your **SUPERPOWER.**

You are Kind

START HERE

If you would like to choose a new mode of transport to take you
to the next part of your magical journey, make your choice now.

To fly on a MAGIC CARPET, turn to page 25
To travel in a PRIVATE JET, turn to page 27
To fly on your own UNICORN, turn to page 29
To travel in a HOT AIR BALLOON, turn to page 31
To travel in a TIME MACHINE, turn to page 33
To use magic INVISIBILITY DUST, turn to page 35
To travel by BOAT, turn to page 37
To fly on a HOVER BOARD, turn to page 39
To fly on a BROOMSTICK, turn to page 41
To travel in a ROCKET, turn to page 43

**If you have completed your magical journey,
Please go to page 186**

Your SUPERPOWER IS......

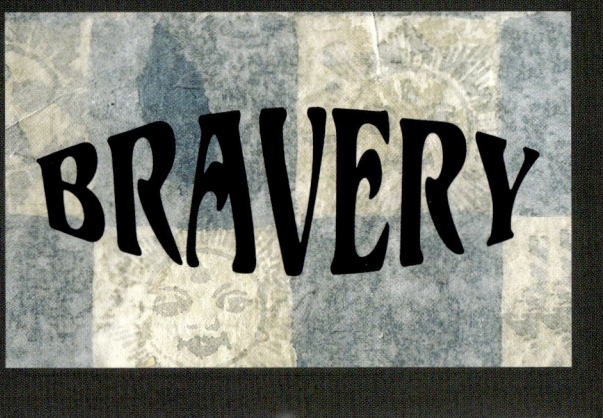

BRAVERY

Look at your SUPERPOWER and feel it inside.
Breathe in and feel the SUPERPOWER starting to work.

Now with your **SUPERPOWER** you can choose to go back through the portal or if you would like to collect more gifts, messages and superpowers, you can continue your adventure in new and exciting lands. If you would like to go back to the portal, take in a deep breath and blow out slowly. Feel yourself disappearing from this magical land and re-appearing back in your room. You may need to try three deep breaths to get you back to the room.

You find a magic key that leads to a room.
In the room is a huge cinema screen.
The curtains are closed.
You notice the curtains slowly opening to
reveal your **SUPERPOWER.**

You are Brave

If you would like to choose a new mode of transport to take you
to the next part of your magical journey, make your choice now.

To fly on a MAGIC CARPET, turn to page 25
To travel in a PRIVATE JET, turn to page 27
To fly on your own UNICORN, turn to page 29
To travel in a HOT AIR BALLOON, turn to page 31
To travel in a TIME MACHINE, turn to page 33
To use magic INVISIBILITY DUST, turn to page 35
To travel by BOAT, turn to page 37
To fly on a HOVER BOARD, turn to page 39
To fly on a BROOMSTICK, turn to page 41
To travel in a ROCKET, turn to page 43

If you have completed your magical journey,
Please go to page 186

Your **SUPERPOWER** IS......

PATIENCE

Look at your SUPERPOWER and feel it inside.
Breathe in and feel the SUPERPOWER starting to work.

Now with your **SUPERPOWER** you can choose to go back through the portal or if you would like to collect more gifts, messages and superpowers, you can continue your adventure in new and exciting lands. If you would like to go back to the portal, take in a deep breath and blow out slowly. Feel yourself disappearing from this magical land and re-appearing back in your room. You may need to try three deep breaths to get you back to the room.

You find a magic key that leads to a room.
In the room is a huge cinema screen.
The curtains are closed.
You notice the curtains slowly opening to
reveal your **SUPERPOWER.**

You are Patient

If you would like to choose a new mode of transport to take you
to the next part of your magical journey, make your choice now.

To fly on a MAGIC CARPET, turn to page 25
To travel in a PRIVATE JET, turn to page 27
To fly on your own UNICORN, turn to page 29
To travel in a HOT AIR BALLOON, turn to page 31
To travel in a TIME MACHINE, turn to page 33
To use magic INVISIBILITY DUST, turn to page 35
To travel by BOAT, turn to page 37
To fly on a HOVER BOARD, turn to page 39
To fly on a BROOMSTICK, turn to page 41
To travel in a ROCKET, turn to page 43

**If you have completed your magical journey,
Please go to page 186**

Your **SUPERPOWER** is......

POSITIVITY

Look at your SUPERPOWER and feel it inside.
Breathe in and feel the SUPERPOWER starting to work.

Now with your **SUPERPOWER** you can choose to go back through the portal or if you would like to collect more gifts, messages and superpowers, you can continue your adventure in new and exciting lands. If you would like to go back to the portal, take in a deep breath and blow out slowly. Feel yourself disappearing from this magical land and re-appearing back in your room. You may need to try three deep breaths to get you back to the room.

You find a magic key that leads to a room.
In the room is a huge cinema screen.
The curtains are closed.
You notice the curtains slowly opening to
reveal your **SUPERPOWER.**

You are Positive

If you would like to choose a new mode of transport to take you
to the next part of your magical journey, make your choice now.

To fly on a MAGIC CARPET, turn to page 25
To fly on a MAGIC CARPET, turn to page 25
To travel in a PRIVATE JET, turn to page 27
To fly on your own UNICORN, turn to page 29
To travel in a HOT AIR BALLOON, turn to page 31
To travel in a TIME MACHINE, turn to page 33
To use magic INVISIBILITY DUST, turn to page 35
To travel by BOAT, turn to page 37
To fly on a HOVER BOARD, turn to page 39
To fly on a BROOMSTICK, turn to page 41
To travel in a ROCKET, turn to page 43

**If you have completed your magical journey,
Please go to page 186**

Your SUPERPOWER *is.....*

RESOURCEFULNESS

**Look at your SUPERPOWER and feel it inside.
Breathe in and feel the SUPERPOWER starting to work.**

Now with your **SUPERPOWER** you can choose to go back through the portal or if you would like to collect more gifts, messages and superpowers, you can continue your adventure in new and exciting lands. If you would like to go back to the portal, take in a deep breath and blow out slowly. Feel yourself disappearing from this magical land and re-appearing back in your room. You may need to try three deep breaths to get you back to the room.

You find a magic key that leads to a room.
In the room is a huge cinema screen.
The curtains are closed.
You notice the curtains slowly opening
to reveal your **SUPERPOWER.**

You are Resourceful

If you would like to choose a new mode of transport to take you
to the next part of your magical journey, make your choice now.

To fly on a MAGIC CARPET, turn to page 25
To travel in a PRIVATE JET, turn to page 27
To fly on your own UNICORN, turn to page 29
To travel in a HOT AIR BALLOON, turn to page 31
To travel in a TIME MACHINE, turn to page 33
To use magic INVISIBILITY DUST, turn to page 35
To travel by BOAT, turn to page 37
To fly on a HOVER BOARD, turn to page 39
To fly on a BROOMSTICK, turn to page 41
To travel in a ROCKET, turn to page 43

If you have completed your magical journey,
Please go to page 186

Your SUPERPOWER IS......

GENEROSITY

Look at your SUPERPOWER and feel it inside.
Breathe in and feel the SUPERPOWER starting to work.

Now with your **SUPERPOWER** you can choose to go back through the portal or if you would like to collect more gifts, messages and superpowers, you can continue your adventure in new and exciting lands. If you would like to go back to the portal, take in a deep breath and blow out slowly. Feel yourself disappearing from this magical land and re-appearing back in your room. You may need to try three deep breaths to get you back to the room.

You find a magic key that leads to a room.
In the room is a huge cinema screen.
The curtains are closed.
You notice the curtains slowly opening
to reveal your **SUPERPOWER.**

You are Generous

START HERE

If you would like to choose a new mode of transport to take you
to the next part of your magical journey, make your choice now.

To fly on a MAGIC CARPET, turn to page 25
To travel in a PRIVATE JET, turn to page 27
To fly on your own UNICORN, turn to page 29
To travel in a HOT AIR BALLOON, turn to page 31
To travel in a TIME MACHINE, turn to page 33
To use magic INVISIBILITY DUST, turn to page 35
To travel by BOAT, turn to page 37
To fly on a HOVER BOARD, turn to page 39
To fly on a BROOMSTICK, turn to page 41
To travel in a ROCKET, turn to page 43

If you have **completed** your **magical** journey,
Please go to page 186

Your SUPERPOWER IS......

COURAGE

Look at your SUPERPOWER and feel it inside.
Breathe in and feel the SUPERPOWER starting to work.

Now with your **SUPERPOWER** you can choose to go back through the portal or if you would like to collect more gifts, messages and superpowers, you can continue your adventure in new and exciting lands. If you would like to go back to the portal, take in a deep breath and blow out slowly. Feel yourself disappearing from this magical land and re-appearing back in your room. You may need to try three deep breaths to get you back to the room.

You find a magic key that leads to a room.
In the room is a huge cinema screen.
The curtains are closed.
You notice the curtains slowly opening
to reveal your **SUPERPOWER.**

You are Courageous

If you would like to choose a new mode of transport to take you
to the next part of your magical journey, make your choice now.

To fly on a MAGIC CARPET, turn to page 25
To travel in a PRIVATE JET, turn to page 27
To fly on your own UNICORN, turn to page 29
To travel in a HOT AIR BALLOON, turn to page 31
To travel in a TIME MACHINE, turn to page 33
To use magic INVISIBILITY DUST, turn to page 35
To travel by BOAT, turn to page 37
To fly on a HOVER BOARD, turn to page 39
To fly on a BROOMSTICK, turn to page 41
To travel in a ROCKET, turn to page 43

If you have completed your magical journey,
Please go to page 186

Cave of Calm
maze of miracles
Magical mountain
castle of creativity
shimmering sea...
ancient island
Whispering grassland...
Den of Dreams...
Room of Rest...
Lake of Enchantment
Hut of Happiness
Rainbow waterfall...
Woods of mystery...
Palace of Peace
Tower of Power...
unknown wilderness
Well of wishes
secret garden
House of Hearts
sleepy stream...

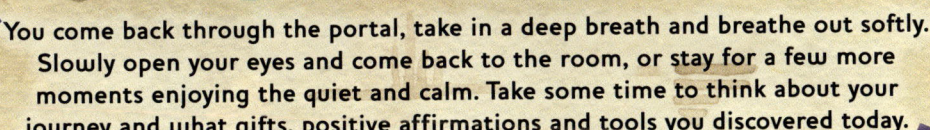

You come back through the portal, take in a deep breath and breathe out softly. Slowly open your eyes and come back to the room, or stay for a few more moments enjoying the quiet and calm. Take some time to think about your journey and what gifts, positive affirmations and tools you discovered today.

This is not

THE END

This is just the beginning of your life adventure.
Go through life picking up messages, clues, signs and lessons on how to stay on the right path, follow your heart and dreams and lead the best life ever.

Anytime, you wish to start another journey, turn to page 3 (the portal page), to begin your new magical adventure.

Remember life is an adventure and wonderful treasure hunt.
Have fun!

relax Kids

A selection of calming audios, visualization stories and affirmation tools for children of all ages.

Relax Kids Audios

Online Downloads

Affirmation Cards

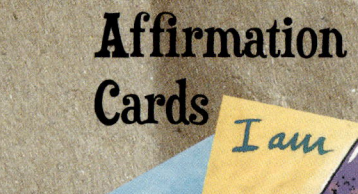

RELAX KIDS RANGE OF BOOKS

Little Book of Stars - *Helping children see their true star quality with simple visualization exercises. The Little Book of Stars is the perfect way to introduce toddlers to relaxation and meditation. Each page explores a positive quality or value in an easy to understand and child friendly way.*

How To Be Happy - *How to be Happy is a scrap book bursting with positive ideas, simple and economical activities and fun games. Each page includes colorful pictures and diagrams to explain the activity in simple child-like language. There are some in-book activities but this is mainly a book of ideas. This book is full of interesting ways to relax, have fun and be happy.*

Aladdins Magic Carpet - *This book combines well-known and loved fairytales with simple meditation and mindfulness techniques to help children relax. Children go on magical adventures in their mind as they imagine they are Aladdin floating on a carpet, Jack climbing the beanstalk and floating in the clouds, the little mermaid swimming in the ocean and Sleeping Beauty lying in a satin bed.*

The Wishing Star - *The Wishing Star is full of creative visualizations, meditations and relaxations. Children can imagine they are lying in soft grass, sitting in a peaceful cave, watching a beautiful sunset and flying like a bird. The book is full of deep body relaxations, lovely nature inspired visualizations and fantasy story meditations.*

Pants Of Peace - *An innovative book that helps children get in touch with a wide range of inner qualities and values through creative meditation and affirmations exercises. Examples include shoe of confidence, cloak of protection, pen of appreciation and hat of happiness.*

The Magic Box - *The Magic Box is full of creative visualizations, meditations and relaxations. Children can imagine they are on a tropical island, flying into space, in a hot air balloon, time travelling and leaving their worries on the worry tree.*

Be Brilliant - *A coloring and activity book that is full of joy and positivity. Children will enjoy cutting out affirmation cards and playing games that promote self esteem and confidence.*

A Monster Handbook - *An interactive part work book, part activity toolkit that helps children tame and train their monster emotions. The Monster Handbook is written in a scrap book style and is bursting with positive exercises and activities to help children understand and work with their emotions.*

7 steps to relaxation

Move — warm up exercises for energy and fun

Play — mindful games for creativity and concentration

Stretch — for balance and inner strength

Feel — peer/self massage for self awareness, empathy and respect

Breathe — for anxiety and inner calm

Believe — or self esteem, confidence and positivity

Relax — for imagination

Use our online class finder to find a class near you!

www.relaxkids.com

TEACH
Relax Kids

Would you like to help children manage stress and anxiety and feel amazing? Teach Relax Kids! Mindfulness and activity classes for children.

For further info:

training@relaxkids.com

www.facebook.com/groups/RKtraining

You can also book online
www.relaxkids.com

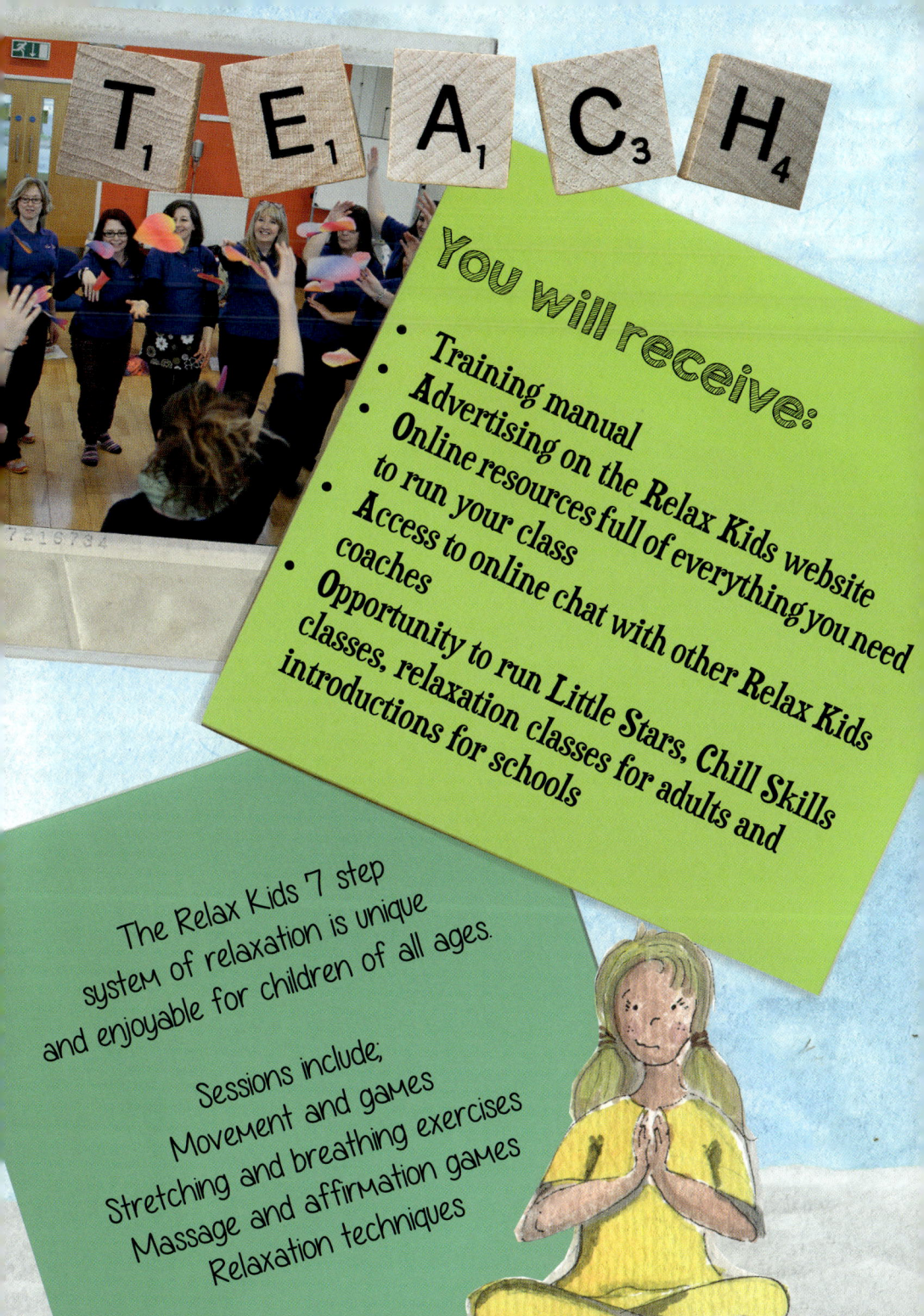

T E A C H

You will receive:

- Training manual
- Advertising on the Relax Kids website
- Online resources full of everything you need to run your class
- Access to online chat with other Relax Kids coaches
- Opportunity to run Little Stars, Chill Skills classes, relaxation classes for adults and introductions for schools

The Relax Kids 7 step system of relaxation is unique and enjoyable for children of all ages.

Sessions include;
Movement and games
Stretching and breathing exercises
Massage and affirmation games
Relaxation techniques

"*This book is wonderful because you get to choose where you want to go, how you want to get there and who you want to meet. The illustrations are inspirational as they help you on your own magical mystery journey. Every time I go on this journey, I feel really adventurous and it helps stretch my imagination. The book has given me lots of ideas for my own stories. I like that it never ends and it goes on and on and on and on and on and on and on and on and on and on....*"
Phoebe Valentine, age 8

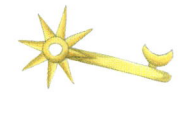

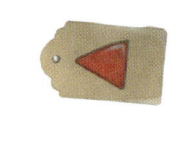

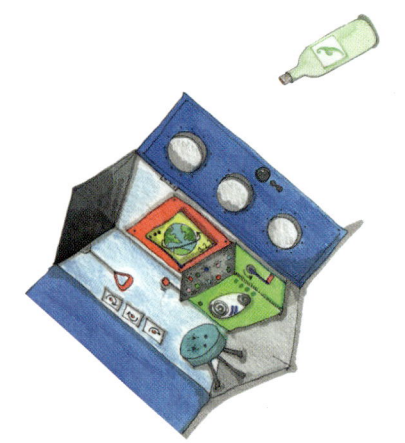

Try Relax Kids for Free!

www.relaxkids.com/freepack

**OUR STREET
BOOKS**

Our Street Books for children of all ages, deliver a potent mix of fantastic, rip-roaring adventure and fantasy stories to excite the imagination; spiritual fiction to help the mind and the heart grow; humorous stories to make the funny bone grow; historical tales to evolve interest; and all manner of subjects that stretch imagination, grab attention, inform, inspire and keep the pages turning. Our subjects include Non-fiction and Fiction, Fantasy and Science Fiction, Religious, Spiritual, Historical, Adventure, Social Issues, Humour, Folk Tales and more.